Visions of Love

James Barnes

Visions of Love

First Edition, May 2013.

ISBN 978-0-9576519-0-6

Cover Design: Emma Denson

Published by

White Light Productions

Horsham, West Sussex, RH12 4DW, U.K.

www.thewhitelights.co.uk

Distributed by

Lulu Press, Inc.

www.lulu.com

For my friends

A labour of love.

May all your highest dreams be fulfilled.

Foreword

For those of you who have never met me, a little introduction will prove helpful. This book is an invitation to a journey into becoming love. It is not simply a conceptual, romantic or theorizing work, but one born of a spiritual vision – of a people fully alive in the love we have been created to carry. I am attempting to voice the heart of God as it has been revealed to me in a fresh way. These writings are a visionary picture, a holy blueprint, and as such are not saturated in years of wisdom from living this out. I would have much rather written from deep life experience – having *worked it all through*, and maybe one day I will be graced with that ability. My prayer is simple: that these thoughts are seeds sown to raise an army, given wholly for love, justice and mercy.

I have written this book firstly as a gift to my friends, and for sure it is written primarily for those who already know Jesus: in the hope of stirring our hearts to love, and in order that all may know that they are free to *simply love*. We can now set ourselves fully on realising these beautiful dreams that are ever before our eyes.

I have used the scriptures in both a creative and liberal fashion, but I believe all rings true with the spirit of the Word. No doubt: if you desire to do God's will, you will have discernment regarding the truth (Jn.7:17, 2 Tim.2:7). My intention is to open a window that reveals how love can be weaved into the fabric of absolutely everything, and as such I have laboured the points of love to the fullest extent, somewhat repetitiously – not being able to shake my thorough nature. Forgive me! As a consequence, this work is better received as a collection of discrete writings than a coherent whole, a series of essays on the love of God. My recommendation therefore is to read it over a season rather than a short intensive period. I wonder if framing it as a series of brief meditations for contemplation would have been a more beneficial approach...

Many of the phrases and expressions I have used herein have already been captured in my songs. I am an artist and as such will seek to express my thoughts in a multitude of ways; the book for sure was not my first choice! I must confess I find the *printed word* format a difficult beast to master – to communicate the full strength and expression of heart, to build living pictures, and not to be constrained by linear styles, perhaps I am not such a natural writer!

I have used The Amplified Bible as my primary source for scriptural quotations. If you are unfamiliar with this translation, I sincerely recommend studying it for a season. In some of the quotations the expansions have been removed for ease of reading, and I have indicated this with a *. I also wish to clarify – there are a few instances in which I have made a statement that includes a reference verse, where the verse marks a close reference point validating the idea, but the statement is not intended to be a retranslation of the verse.

Whilst I could take the time for every quote: to consider which Biblical translation renders the intended meaning best, there is only so much time in a day! Having thoroughly reviewed this work, I believe there is very little (if any) detriment to both the clarity and sentiment of what is being said through the use of the one translation. There is one further reason for using the Amplified translation: its' ability to communicate the strength of spiritual realities in accord with our experiences. Both the energy and sheer depth of truths can so often be lost through our simplified language; though in this case we may be sacrificing the flow and concise articulation that word for word translations carry.

I also take the view that experiences greatly aid wisdom. I wonder how deep our insights can ever be absent practical experiences? If we consider how we construct our worldviews, perspectives and theology, a lack of experience should not be the basis (for determining possibilities). At the foundation, we take the Word of God as our source, holding its authenticity in the highest regard. Together with the Word, we embrace a determination to continue to believe for that which we do not yet see (Rom.4), balancing the tension of present and potential reality. Truths in their full maturity are then grounded in practical wisdom - what does this look like in practice? How does humanity connect with this? What are the steps we can take to live out and fully realize these truths? And lastly we consider - is our perspective holistic and complete? If principles are not fully thought through and worked out, we can be left with partial truths, forming the basis for common misconceptions. Holding all of this in view, my aim has been to draw conclusions based on the convergence of life experience and the complete counsel of God, in order to create a clear map for what is possible with Him (Acts 20:27).

One final note: If God speaks to you regarding any of the revelations detailed herein, in any way – whether key points, clarification, life experience; I would love to enter into dialogue on this and journey in love with all who wish to. If you feel inspired to create something based on the text or wish to collaborate on a creative project please contact me!

- What does a life of love look like? -

Context

For some time now, the message of love has been burning on my heart, and these last few years I've been longing to bring this message into a wider sphere. Being spurred on by the Holy Spirit, my friends and the power of the truth He has revealed, I am compelled by the potential of a collective submersed in love. God desires a people and *a family* to dwell with, not just a collection of fiery individuals. Many have been dreaming of living in heavenly communities for such a long time, yet God has been dreaming of this ever longer! *If we truly get love* – there is more than enough power in this to see all these dreams fulfilled.

The revelations of love's universal purpose and potential have had profound and lasting effects on me. The impact is not dissimilar from the first encounters I had with the Lord – becoming aware of His reality and salvation through Jesus Christ. Seeing *the potency of love* – as the foundation of *why God?!* – In almost every respect validates this depth of impact. It is the core of who He is and all He does. Upon glimpsing this paradigm shifting revelation, we suddenly realise that we truly understand Him deeply and thoroughly, love makes sense of it all.

The fullest expression of His love is as much about love manifest in a community – in all its diversity, as it is about the personal revelation of love between God and an individual. The Father's love must be manifest in all creation! This is our universal mandate from God. In love we find fullness and satisfaction, we yearn for it more than anything else, which is no surprise – we were created by the One who is Love in His very nature. If anyone thinks he knows much of spirituality without love, he is deceived (1 Cor.8:1-3). The truth really is: *God is love* and we too are to become love in every sense in the fullness of time.

In recent years there has begun a great spiritual awakening in the family of God. Being radically sold out for Jesus is becoming a common experience. People are deeply communing with God and crying out for revival. The spiritual awakening that has occurred in these last few decades is truly great, but something so much greater is on the horizon. These outpourings have been an essential season of preparation for a lifestyle of deep personal spirituality. As a consequence a great body of people have become active in supernatural evangelism: prophecy, healing, miraculous prayer. One of the most encouraging signs of change is the renewed reverence for the tangible presence of God. The sense of the imminent move of God is ubiquitous – brewing under the surface, ready to burst at any moment in an explosive river of glorious life.

The movement of love brewing in our hearts is set to eclipse this spiritual awakening. The two are destined to run together and love will take the elements of spiritual revival and make them truly heavenly. Imagine an unparalleled outpouring of love – not just peoples' testimonies of the conviction of God and His truth as in past movements, but multitudes baptised in love and carrying it everywhere they go. His love will sustain this movement and will become the sign to all that Jesus is alive in His people. The effect of love will be greater than any other gift. It is imperative therefore that we both understand and experience the depths of God's love and learn to steward this gift as faithful sons – *giving away freely all of the love that He gives to us.*

My prayer is that a generation of lovers rises out of the presence of the Lord, carrying His living love: the power that draws the whole world into His heart.

Enjoy!

God desires a family to dwell with.

The abundant power in love
Burns the deepest fire in our hearts
Resolute: to see all of our dreams fulfilled.

Brewing under the surface

Ready to burst at any moment
In an explosive river of glorious life

His love will sustain this movement

Giving away freely: all the love He gives us

Love will become the sign to all
that Jesus is alive in His people

The power that draws the whole world
into His heart

the potential of a collective submersed in love

Contents

– The Nature of Love –

To love is the art of living – really living

Love & Life

The principle purpose in our lives is love: to love, be loved, and to know love (Jn.17:3); it is truly life's quintessential element. Love is also the most effective agent at making life happen: it energizes us... *Love creates life*. People who are *'full of life'* often have that spark about them, *"I love life!"* they cry as they ooze energy and excitement about the future – brimming over with possibilities, there is very little that can pull them down. Love is not just the origin of physical life, but the source of spiritual and emotional life as well. Wherever we find true love amongst people, the substance and energy of life is ever present and it empowers all who come into contact with it.

People feel most alive when *in love*, and whilst it is a common belief that this is true only of romantic engagements, this is not so. We experience the same life-joy (and more so!) when living in the love of God. Such an experience cannot be contained by an individual, and the love and life begins to effect people all around. The loving atmosphere found amidst a close community is so valuable that people crave it their whole lives – especially if they've had significant experiences of it before. The greatest life we can ever experience in relationships is the active exchange of love. Love is here to draw us into living the fullest lives and to becoming life giving vessels (Jn.10:10, Col.2:10), It also provides the solid foundation for trust. When we know we are genuinely loved by someone we know that they will put our interests first, this enables us to trust them – in fact it is difficult not to trust someone who shows us pure love. The full power of being loved by someone in a pure way is difficult to fathom... Consider the dynamic transformation that will occur when a collective determines to love a particular individual at every turn, how free will they become? *How much power is there in the love of God?!*

Truly His love is the purest, and when we find it, we arrive upon a profound awareness of the meaning of our lives. When we know the love and acceptance of God (just as we are!) we are liberated from introspection and egocentrism. We find ourselves wrapped in security and freedom in love's compelling atmosphere, insecurities exist only where love does not abound – and we are losing them all! We find ourselves pilgrims on the selfless journey, our perspective set focused outwards – upon others. As we are transformed more completely into the nature of Christ and as we abide in His presence, selflessness becomes our permanent abode. We become so full of His love that there is no empty place left in our souls. Perhaps this emptiness we sometimes feel is simply the absence of love? *(fill it God!)* One day we will truly say: *the love of Christ compels us!* – And all the time we are propelled on by the real substance of love, we will never become overtired of serving others; we will not be able to act only from a place of duty when the desire of heaven is moving us, we will love helping people!

Knowing we are loved makes us free

"I am zealous for you with a godly eagerness and a divine jealousy."

2 Cor.11:2

"But I am afraid that, as the serpent deceived Eve by his craftiness, your minds will be led astray from the simplicity and purity of devotion to Christ"

2 Cor.11:3, NASB

Simple, Yet Powerful

Love starts with God: He is love. He is light and life. He lives by expressing His nature – being Himself as it were. Who He is, is what He does, and He is love through and through.

We start this journey by receiving a gift of reconciliation to God through the life and love of Jesus Christ. In Him we have all we need. He is the source of all our love. Love truly is our sole purpose and the most glorious victory of all. It enables us to see clearly what is of true value – what really matters (Phil.1:9 10). Love teaches us to assign the right level of emphasis on truth and action: to rightly divide the truth (2 Tim.2:15) and to see the importance and relevance of each nuance. The truth is not complicated. Until love is fully formed in us, we can be distracted with side issues, things of lesser importance; we cannot long be distracted when love is at the centre of our hearts. There are many well meaning folks travelling around these days, offering all kinds of teachings and fresh ideas, but many have missed His heart. We are simply *trying to follow Jesus* – and love Him – nothing more, nothing less. There is no great secret or hidden teaching that we need: we simply need to know Him and to love. When love is *fully come* our focus stays true and the more we love the clearer we see (Prov.4:18). We are to walk true to what we already know (Phil.3:16). The fullness of love is the fullness of maturity (Eph.3:17-19), this is what we attain to – not to some other abstract notion of godliness, spirituality or religious practices etc. The word for perfection in the New Covenant is the same word for maturity (teleios), so let us walk as mature sons (Rom.8:14), and let us walk in love.

To love is to simply give of ourselves; it is a gift we can all give. Love helps in whatever way – willing to help regardless of what is needed, willing to play any role without strings attached (without the pride of choosing how we desire to give). God in His wisdom created a world, where *the one gift that is the most important is the one that we can all give* – and the one that we all need. The exchange of love knits our hearts together (Col.2:2), this is His genius! God intends that all have the opportunity to follow Him whole heartedly, not based on our natural gifts and intelligence. A gift expressed in love is its ultimate expression, and love will always go further than simply gift. The limit on how much we can love people is only the limit of our time and resources. God can expand our hearts to love as many as come to us, if we will keep our hearts fixed on Him.

Following Jesus is simple, but very costly. In our pride, we often cloud issues and make them complicated, the effect can be to distract from the hard decisions facing us or the reality that our hearts aren't surrendered to God. In obedience we find simplicity, if we come to the kingdom as a child (simply trusting and obeying), He will grant us the grace to do all things through Christ who strengthens us (Phil.4:13).

There is a simple question we have often considered – *how much difference would a lot more love make to everything?*

We cannot long be distracted

when love is at the centre of our hearts

The most important gift in life

is one we can all give

Mercy, Mercy, Mercy...

The incredible power in His love is found in the unending nature of His mercy during our time on earth. To me He has been the most patient, faithful and committed lover beyond my imagination: *"His mercies are new every morning"* (Lam.3:22-23). One cannot overstate how profound the experience of this truth is. Perhaps the most striking description of His extreme grace to us is found in Romans 5, the Amplified captures it best: (albeit a little wordy)

"... God's free gift is not at all to be compared to the trespass [His grace is out of all proportion to the fall of man]. For if many died through one man's falling away, much more profusely did God's grace and the free gift [that comes] through the undeserved favour of the one Man Jesus Christ abound and overflow to and for [the benefit of] many. Nor is the free gift at all to be compared to the effect of that one [man's] sin. For the sentence [following the trespass] of one [man] brought condemnation, whereas the free gift [following] many transgressions brings justification. For if because of one man's trespass death reigned through that one, much more surely will those who receive [God's] overflowing grace (unmerited favour) and the free gift of righteousness [putting them into right standing with Himself] reign as kings in life through the one Man Jesus Christ."

Rom.5:15-17

It continues a little further

"But then law came in, [only] to expand and increase the trespass [making it more apparent and exciting opposition]. But where sin increased and abounded, grace (God's unmerited favour) has surpassed it and increased the more and superabounded." v**20**.

- Selah -

So...

What does this all mean? And - *Does it really say that?*

How many times do I need to read it before I get it?!

The grace of God revealed in this Great Covenant is actually so incredible, that it cannot be compared with the sin and destruction that has been released on the earth through the fall of man; we cannot even put *the grace of God* and *the sin of all mankind* on the same scale. To the heart that has not yet been awakened to the pure revelations of His grace the world certainly doesn't look this way at present! Perhaps this is also a reference to our becoming a *new creation,* a new breed as it were, so profoundly different that our newfound life in Christ has the potential to be *entirely* unlike our past. He even goes as far as to say that – as surely and universally as sin and destruction are experienced by all, even more surely will those who enter into this covenant of grace – *reign as kings in life,* and – *where sin has abounded, grace has surpassed it!* No one could seriously attempt to question the presence of sin and destruction that occurs throughout the earth or the effect is has had on all people, resulting in injustice, poverty, sickness, etc.. Our expectation and experience of grace is to become so great that we *anticipate grace more strongly than sin and death*. Could this be why love hopes in all things? We know that God works all things to our good (Rom.8:28), and that He has an incredible way of turning almost anything around for His glory! At the very least we can empathise more effectively with others in the midst of the most unjust sufferings (2 Cor.1:4). There is even a grace to overcome every temptation (1 Cor.10:13). Furthermore, this very grace – His long-suffering – is salvation to us! (2 Pet.3:9, 15). Anyone who has walked with the Lord for any significant length of time knows how profoundly true this is for us all! He has even inspired us to offer the same mercy and longsuffering – becoming gracious beyond the rational, knowing that it empowers others to do likewise. Love truly covers a multitude of sins!

His gift of grace

Cannot be compared with sin and its effects...

His grace is off the chart

If we consider the implication of this grace, we see that His love is also out of all proportion to our mistakes, perhaps this is one of the most difficult things for us to realise and accept – not least because it sounds like a *romantic fairytale!* All I know is, the more days I walk, the more profoundly impacting and the more overwhelming is His love and grace toward me – to the point where I am often speechless and in awe, *deeply in awe,* constantly amazed by the radical nature of His heart. I don't mean to paint a picture of life which sounds like it is free of trials, mistakes or things going wrong; what I am trying to communicate is that His love towards us is *so* much greater – and this is what we begin to see, *far more* than the difficulties and errors that we make. Anyone who offers *once for all* to wipe the slate completely clean, forgiving everything we have done wrong and at the same time bringing us to completeness in Him is more than extraordinary – surely only God! (Heb.10:14, 2:15 – and will He not allow us to start over again and again? Did His grace stop short of refreshing us every time we need it?) And thank God *all means all!!!* My experiences of the strength of love have stripped me of every doubt, and I feel with certainty – *He would do it all again for us (the cross!) – a hundred times if need be!* Fortunately His wisdom made sure He fixed it once for all!

But God – so rich is He in His mercy!

Eph.2:4

Your grace sets the heart free to cries of
Not guilty! Not guilty!

I love how Jesus put it so aptly when he said: *"...her sins, many [as they are], are forgiven her –because she has loved much. But he who is forgiven little loves little"* (Lk.7:47). When we see how overwhelming and numerous our sins were in the eyes of God, set against a backdrop of such great love that offers us forgiveness of all – (even putting our sins forever beyond our reach from here on, Ps.103:12) – seeing this incredible gift of absolute forgiveness undoes our hearts and stirs the deepest of loves in pure gratitude.

"For I desire mercy, not sacrifice and the knowledge of God more than all burnt offerings."

Hos.6:6, RSV

The Sign of Jesus

Love is to become one of the primary signs attesting to the truth of Jesus' resurrection and a distinguishing mark of the lives of His followers (Jn.13:35). It is my belief that the love of God manifest in the earth will draw more people to God than anything else. It has the ability to transcend all boundaries and unify people across cultures, traditions and belief systems. When all else fails to unite people love succeeds. It is a marvel – almost a miracle, that Christians have been so divided thus far. Christ has once for all fully united us, becoming our peace, making us actually one in Him and breaking down every wall that previously divided us (Eph.2:14-16, 18). *For you are all one in Christ Jesus* and *Christ is all and in all* (Gal.3:28, Col.3:11).

"By this all men will know that you are my disciples, if you have love for one another."

Jn.13:35

He doesn't simply say, 'by this, some men will know that you are my disciples.' The statement is profoundly clear – all men *will* know that you are my disciples – *if* you have love for one another. ***All men!***

If we take the Discovery Bible as our reference for grammar, we find the following: the emphasis falls on *all men* and *My* disciples. 'Know' refers to personal experiential knowledge, and the love is a habitual, continual love – agapē: the pure, unselfish, deep love. So to paraphrase Jesus, All men will have a personal experience of the followers of Jesus (who are just like Him!) if we walk continually in love toward one another. Will they also see that we have been with the real living Jesus? (Acts 4:13).

Love releases spiritual light.

"Whoever loves his brother lives in the light."

1 John

The book of *1 John* is perhaps the simplest summary of the Covenant we have with God through Christ. John, more than any of the other apostles, carries the clear message of love in His writings. Since John writes so much about love, it is helpful to examine what he says:

God loved us first and initiated a relationship with us (Jn.15:16), now we love because He first loved us – *because of the love He has given to us* (1 Jn.4:19). Love is from God and he who loves is born of God and is coming to know and understand Him (4:7). He who dwells in love dwells in God (4:12, 16). God's nature abides in those who abide in Him (1 Jn.3:9). To love God is to obey Him perfectly in maturity (2:5, 3:24). If anyone loves the world: love for the Father is not in him (2:15) – these two cannot coexist – if anyone loves the Father, love for the world will die. Whoever loves his brother lives in the light (2:10), this is true spiritual light – *love releases spiritual light.*

How light will the world become around us when all we do is love?

Continuing...

The connection between love and life – we know that we have passed over out of death into life by the fact that we love the brethren, he who does not love abides in death (3:14). One of the signs of someone truly born of the

Spirit is their love for the family of God. His Spirit is also the evidence that we abide in Him (4:13). The sign of love is laying down our lives (3:16). We should love one another just as He has commanded us (3:23). The love of God *cannot* abide in us if we do not act in compassion, generosity and in support of those in need (3:17). If we love God, we will love our brother – these two always come together (4:20), i.e. if we learn to love God truly, the consequence will always be – our actively loving others and them knowing our love for them. We come to know that we love the children of God – when we love God and obey His commands (5:2, 3), this is one of the most interesting statements of all and is often overlooked. John says that when we obey God and love Him, we become aware of our love for our brothers and sisters in Christ. This is one of few verses that indicate that we should focus first on loving God as the way to outwork love for others most effectively. For the love of God is this: that we do His commands (5:3), and His commands are not a burden to us!

Love breaks the back of the mundane...

"Where your treasure is, there will your heart be also."

Lk.12:34

Becoming Love

If God is our supreme treasure, He will also become the permanent abode of our heart. We know that what we focus on is what we become, and that gazing upon the glory of the Lord transforms us into His nature (2 Cor.3:18). He is so keen for us to gaze with open hearts! He is committed to releasing fresh love to us because He knows the effect that it has – He is sowing the seeds that transform us into His likeness. The more we see His love, the more that we will love like Him. By walking with love, we become love – just spending time with Him. As we dwell in His presence love will become the abode of the heart, i.e. love *will* take over if we stay there.

His gaze has stolen my eyes away

Jesus teaches us to *abide in Him* – to dwell in love and to abide in His Word. In the eyes of Jesus, following Him is a constant pursuit. Abiding is a constant leaning of our heart into the Lord, always being aware, ready and available for His interventions. In some translations of John 15:4 the phrase *Remain in me* is used, which seems the most appropriate for the analogy of a *continual abiding* in the vine. If we keep relating to Him and following every nudge of His heart we will bear the most fruit. He teaches us how to abide in His love, so that both His joy and ours are full (Jn.15:11) – *we find fullness of joy as love abides!* Furthermore, His anointing teaches us to abide – *in the anointing* (1 Jn.2:27) If we love one another God abides in us, and His love has been perfected in us (1 Jn.4:12, NKJV – we cannot separate loving others and full maturity in God), there is no obstruction to His presence and He wills to abide tangibly. It is a marvel the presence of God does not abide with us constantly! The sustaining grace of a continual outpouring of love (a love anointing as it were), comes only from a place of abiding in God.

"The father has not left me alone, for I always do what pleases him."

Jn.8:29

Why am I focusing so strongly on abiding? *Jesus did.* It is essential that we learn what it really means to abide. Jesus said – *"the Father abiding in me does the works"* (Jn.14:10). Those who utter caution to extended prayer cannot deny that abiding yields the very works of God, for Jesus said such! He also relates it to our established freedom: *"If you abide in My word, you are truly My disciples and you will know the Truth and the Truth will set you free"* (Jn.8:31-32*, 36 – *Free indeed!* Gal.5:1– *Completely liberated*). People love to quote the end result – *the Truth will set you free,* without the strategy as to how we get there! It is my conviction that when Jesus is teaching on abiding, He also means for us to walk continually in what He has already taught us, and to be ready to receive the further truth He wishes to bring to us in the future. Is He not saying – *keep on listening to me – whatever comes, keep on listening and following what I am teaching you...?*

There is a connection between what we abide in and what is continually present in our lives. Abiding is a covenant concept (Jn.6:56) and is found in our communion. We begin first by consecrating ourselves: finding a place of deep and thorough repentance – re-evaluating our entire value system in the light of God and receiving the power of the Holy Spirit in order to walk this new life out. The question of how we then stand in this place is a crucial one. Sensing the call of God to absolute surrender, and the desire to be fully His; we have sought many times to give ourselves wholly to God, although later our hearts have wandered off. Our abiding in Him will take care of our consecrated walk before Him. The wisdom of abiding in Him will open wide the doors of heaven and keep these precious hearts set on His face.

So how are we to abide? He has taught us that *"He is a rewarder of those who diligently seek Him"* (Heb.11:6), that we will not progress far without discipline (proverbs!), faith and patience (Heb.6:12), and He even says, *"if you keep my commandments you will abide in my love"* – **obedience!** We can seek Him with every sure expectation, for it is His good pleasure to give us the kingdom (Lk.12:32), even every good gift (Jam.1:17), and He gives the Holy Spirit to those who obey Him! (Acts 5:32).

Love is calling...

Are we listening?

His heart to us is resoundingly clear: His will is for us to live in His love and to become the constant outpouring of it, so that we collectively carry and share an authentic *love culture* first and foremost. He *passionately* desires this for our lives – *not just a little!* Since we are aware of this, we can ask in faith for the revelation of it to us and through us, fully confident that He will.

While writing this I became aware of an invitation from the Father: if we want to enter deeper into His love, we can start by *loving on Him* a lot more (2 Sam.22:26); this *love movement* will be carried by those who inhabit that place of loving on Him daily and who find their rest in the place of being *in love* with Him...

As we dwell in His presence

love becomes the abode of the heart.

We have previously visited the following notion – one of the greatest doorways into the experience of transformation into the nature of Christ is by *beholding His glory* (2 Cor.3:18). A striking aspect of this dynamic that we observe over and over is the tendency for us all to exhibit the specific characteristics of His nature that we have encountered. God reveals Himself to us in various forms all the time, relating to us in a multitude of different ways. He comes to us as our Teacher, our Shepherd, our Father... We find that as we experience the Shepherd we start to take on the nature of *The Shepherd*, by imitating what we see. The Shepherd causes us to be sensitive to pastoral issues – caring for the needs of the saints, listening, guiding. The Father causes the Spirit of adoption to come forth in us: the desire to make a home for His children, the care for all the saints. The Lord's intention for us all is for us to deeply know the whole spectrum of His faces and forms and therefore to take on the full diversity of His characteristics and ways. As we mature in God we walk closer to the line that Jesus took; rather than simply exuding the traits of our characteristic defaults, (say being prophetic a great deal of the time, but lacking the pastoral); we act according to the Holy Spirit's guidance in manifesting the diverse characteristics of God. Jesus walked not just as *The Prophet*, but Priest and King, Shepherd, Lover... He manifested the *very name of God* (Jn.17:26) – *revealing who God is* – to such we are called!

The greatest legacy in life is to become like God.

If this is all that our lives amount to, then we have done very well!

The Greatest Depths

Paul knew so strongly and thoroughly the love of God, that he was persuaded of its universal pre-eminence beyond all doubt (Rom.8:38-39 – i.e. He knew that he knew that he knew he was loved!) How thoroughly can the love of God be revealed to us? In this experience His soul was in the most secure place it can ever be. He trusted God and His love for Him. It is like the trust of a child in loving parents: when you know you are loved to the point that it generates trust in you. It is an ease of faith without striving and this is partly how we know with certainty God will reveal it – *because we need it* and it produces faith in us... Paul knew – **nothing can separate us from His love.** In reality, nothing could ever happen that would cause Paul to doubt the love of God even slightly – any trial, any misfortune that was difficult to understand, it did not matter what would come that would attempt to question God's love, he could not doubt it anymore. How do I know that this is what he was referring to and that we can experience the same today? Because I know people who are alive today who do experience this! **God show us!**

Is it surprising that the place of communion with God brings our soul into a total rest and peace beyond words and understanding? Especially when we see the connection between God's presence and rest? (Ex.33:14)

Nothing can separate us from His love

There is even a place we can come to in prayer, where we pray until love takes over and is established as the fountain of our hearts. We walk from this place of prayer carrying the essence of love and people all around us are profoundly impacted.

Our lives are a love story

What will we create?

The Romance

To love Him truly is all. To love Him is the way to become like Him, *love opens the heart* – this is why worship is key, and we know – "where your treasure is, there will your heart be," i.e. *what you love is where you live.*

A heart addicted to love

Carries a holiness unlike another

We know that *holy* means to be *'set apart.'* The purest love will keep itself devoted for one lover – this is commitment and faithfulness, this is purity. Holiness can be considered as *love expressed as a lifestyle (in the key choices).* Knowing the uniquely precious aspect of a heart kept for just one: we choose to keep that which is most precious to share only with them. Spiritual holiness is found in keeping our hearts wholly for God. By it we guard the thoughts and intents of our hearts; this is found in the discipline of what we look upon, think about, give our heart to: in all the choices we make. True holiness is a positive focused passion, centred on love. And what would be special in a marriage if it were not for the intimacy, affection and closeness of hearts? If marriage is a symbol of our union with God, how much more powerful and significant is this dynamic we find in deep intimacy with God? Are we not to anticipate the deepest union that we can ever experience with another to be with God? In light of this, I wish for all to be free to pursue the open hearted intimate times with the Lord regularly, how can we not long for deep prayer?!

You are the greatest gift that You have given me

Being with You is greater than all Your promises
Greater than all in this life.

We have found that romance and the arts are intertwined - *the arts are so often the expression and connection of hearts.* All who know well the ways of *romance* know that the very essence of romance – *the expression of the heart and the pursuit of the heart,* is most often found in artistic, spontaneous and unrestrained affections. Is it any wonder then that we find such power tied up in the song? In worship? In the arts? All true worship as being simply *loving on God.* We have greatly underestimated the power of loving on God in whole hearted worship! This also adds credence to our experience that *fresh spontaneous worship from the heart is often the most powerful of all.*

"The Spirit whom He has caused to dwell in us yearns over us and He yearns for the Spirit [to be welcome] with a jealous love."

Jam.4:5

There are glimpses of the extreme love we can feel for God in a few places in scripture:

"Because Your love is better than life, my lips shall praise You."

Ps.63:3, NKJV

The Contemporary English Version is clearer - *"Your love means more than life to me."*

The sense of feeling '*ruined for God*' is here – of knowing Him and His love, literally changing our entire paradigm for life; of desiring Him so strongly that we would gladly lay our lives down just to know Him a little more.

"Set me like a seal upon your heart, like a seal upon your arm; for love is as strong as death, jealousy is as hard and cruel as Sheol. Its flashes are flashes of fire, a most vehement flame! [the very flame of the Lord!] Many waters cannot quench love, neither can floods drown it, if a man would offer all the goods of his house for love, he would be utterly scorned and despised."

SOS.8:6-7

Love burns like blazing fire

- Blazing Fire -

See the flame

God: Restore our first love.

Wrecked for God

There are two principle ways God intends to *wreck us.* Love is the one thing that can ruin us for anything else. First of all we become ruined by our desire to know Him and His love for us – this is becoming quite common place these days! As His love starts to abide in our hearts and takes over, we also become ruined for His love manifest in the lives of others. He desires that we become as committed to sharing Him as to seeking Him – to doing the works and acts of God as interceding for them. There are typically two perspectives on this spectrum, those who seek God first and those who act first in faith; it appears to be a matter of personality, gift and preference as to which we opt for, however – we know that God is seeking to flip our experience as we become more like Jesus. We know that we will not become fully mature without loving one another, obeying God and working His works.

The heart that is ruined for knowing God seeks Him out as food and water, *I must know Him, I must know His heart – be His heart, I can do nothing without Him! One thing I desire...* (Ps.27:4). His desires become ours, and it is no longer I who lives but Christ in me (Gal.2:20). Through *His love in us* our affections for the things of the world have truly died once for all, and now all that resides in us is a consuming desire for Him and for all people to know Him and to know love. We cannot stray far from the awareness that God cares about people so much more than anything else – for Him it is all about them, for Him this world – all of creation is about *Him and us* and His attention is focused on us. Through faith we can access the love He has for every man and begin to release it: the Holy Spirit brews love in us and hope abounds (Rom.5:5). The fullness of His love dwelling in us will result in us loving each other *in the way that He loves us*. This love desires to be all things to all men, to connect with all of them, to establish a real living connection with people; to become and do whatever it takes to build authentic relationship so that love can be received. Paul went so far as to say:

"...although I am free in every way from anyone's control, I have made myself a bond servant to everyone, so that I might gain the more... I have become all things to all men that I might by all means save some."

1 Cor.9:19-22

He continues on...

"Just as I myself strive to please [to accommodate myself to the opinions, desires, and interests of others, adapting myself to] all men in everything I do, not aiming at or considering my own profit and advantage, but that of the many in order that they may be saved."

1 Cor.10:33

Love is the one thing that can ruin us for anything else

"...If one loves God truly, he is known by God."

Rom.8:3*

Intimacy & Obedience

We cannot deny that loving, obeying and following God opens a door to love and intimacy with Him. As we obey Him and walk the paths He walks, both seeing and feeling the very same things – we come to know His heart. Knowing God personally and deeply is the very meaning of life:

"This is eternal life: to know You, the only true and real God, and to know Him, Jesus Christ Whom You have sent."

John 17:3*

It has not escaped our attention that according to Jesus – *eternal life is something to be experienced and enjoyed now.*

Jesus also talked of the experience of those who obey Him, and the reality of God that will be revealed to them:

"The person who has my commands and keeps them is the one who loves me; and whoever loves me will be loved by my father, and I will love him and will show myself to him."

John 14:21*

"If a person loves me, he will keep My word; and My Father will love him, and We will come to him and make our home with him."

John 14:23*

The tangible abiding presence of God will rest upon all who obey and love Him thoroughly and we *will* come to know Him in deep communion; He will show us what He is doing and we will become His very Home. What greater motivation can there be for following His every command?

Is *love* actually the biggest key to release the Holy Spirit?

He has taught us clearly, that we cannot separate the notions of love and obedience just like we cannot separate faith and action; true love will lead to obedience, just like true faith always leads to action – for nothing in our heart will desire anything that will cause Him offence. We can also rest assured in our obedience that He is working all things to our good (Rom.8:28).

Jesus - "...I do as the Father has commanded me, so that the world may know that I love the Father..."

John.14:31*

"The wise in heart will accept and obey commandments"

Pr.10:8

If I Have Not Love, I Am Nothing...

At some point we meditate on 1 Cor.13 and it hits home – *it truly is all about love*, but do I really believe this? Do I live like this is true? Do we see love as truly the most powerful force on earth? Only faith working through love counts for anything (Gal.5:6). When the love journey sprung up afresh in my heart several years ago, God placed these questions before me. How do we respond? We know God is able and willing to make us like Him – in this as much as in anything else – so we pray – Lord, show me this is true, write it on my heart, open my eyes to see it and to believe it like You do, teach me to live in the knowledge that love is the only thing that counts...

But *why?* Asks the inquisitive soul, why is love the essential thing? Surely many good deeds done without love are significant? Surely other things are important and powerful? What is so different about an act done in love versus the same act – even meeting a need, done without love? What is it that makes it love?

I have no doubt that my questions far outweigh my answers; and that to attempt to fully answer these questions is beyond me. I have observed one thing though, that love carries with it the power to transform hearts and that works done in love leave a lasting impression on people. There is definitely something distinct about the substance of love, which we are all conscious of, that both changes and empowers us to walk a different way. We can all recognise a person who carries love overflowing from their heart; we are impacted every time we meet someone like this. Many souls have come to Christ simply by a brief interaction with a heart overflowing with love. How can we doubt His power in this?

"...Earnestly desire and zealously cultivate the greatest and best gifts and graces. And yet I will show you a still more excellent way."

1 Cor.12:31*

His conjecture here is that love is a better way than all other gifts and graces. 1 Cor.13 is preceded and concluded with a strong instruction to *pursue love.* The message is unmistakable. How many times it is quoted – *eagerly desire to prophesy,* and true – but how often – *pursue the love of God as the ultimate quest?!*

"Eagerly pursue and seek to acquire this love

[make it your aim, your great quest]"

1 Cor.14:1

31

Furthermore, we see some striking characteristics of love voiced in 1 Cor.13:

Love hopes all things – why is love such an optimist?

Is it because pessimism is the enemy of opportunity? We know that faith can create opportunities and is also our access door to heaven's resources. The one who knows Him, His heart and His eagerness to move understands just how close these glorious possibilities are before our very eyes – it is hard not to be optimistic when we are aware of this reality! In my experience the Holy Spirit takes such an optimistic perspective (although at times can be a shocking realist!) Maybe He is optimistic because He knows His own heart and power? He knows what He will do! Or as a good friend of mine once remarked, *"Reality is: God can do anything."* When we focus on the Divine we often cannot hold back our optimism, conversely when we put our focus on human nature and the balance of history, it yields a relative pessimism.

Love removes disappointment through the vision of fresh possibilities (the expectation of goodness born in the experience of love, it cannot be discouraged or pulled down by misfortune, perhaps even resting in the grace that liberates us from our trials, it has the energy to overcome disappointments and frustrations – seeing better days ahead and by this refreshing the soul). Whatever has gone before, we see such abundant opportunity each day for great things. So why is love optimistic? Is it because love so wants the best that hope is born? – is it because it enables endurance under all circumstances? There is one thing we know for certain in this regard, we are encouraged to think and meditate upon the positives (Phil.4:8), and such yields a profoundly optimistic perspective.

When we really believe

The greatest thing we can do is love people

How will we live?

"...I am a fundamentalist Christian, I'm fundamentalist to the core,

when it comes to the love thing."

Cornel West

Love becomes profoundly practical...

The Gospel to the Poor

"Then the King will say to those at His right hand, Come, you blessed of My Father, inherit the kingdom prepared for you from the foundation of the world. For I was hungry and you gave me food, I was thirsty and you gave Me something to drink, I was a stranger and you brought Me together with yourselves and welcomed and entertained and lodged Me. I was naked and you clothed Me, I was sick and you visited Me with help and ministering care, I was in prison and you came to see Me... Truly I tell you, in so far as you did it for one of the least of these My brethren, you did it for Me."

Mt.25:35-40

Firstly, to consider our context: the contrast between first and third world is probably among the greatest of contrasts in all the world. That such a world could exist and that the people of the West have not risen up and found a way to overturn this state of affairs is astonishing. Any discussion of love, without considering the plight of those in greatest need would miss one of its central foundations; as such I could not detach this discussion from the chapter focused on the nature of love. My aim here is not to discuss the sizable systemic issues as to why this extreme disparity exists and how such an unjust global system could arise. Any attempt here would no doubt fail as a gross oversimplification, I could not do it justice – I take it as a given that the situation is well understood by all due to the free and wide availability of information, stats and documentation.

A few years ago I was graced with the opportunity to see what love looks like in one of the world's poorest places. When living amongst the poorest, the opportunities to give welcome help are so numerous that the key questions and decisions we face are focused on resources and are about prioritising need – where to start and where *not* to help, rather than the struggle of finding an open door (as among the rich). Where the poor have nothing, it is ever so easy to give. Many do not even have family, let alone provision – so even spending a little time caring for someone can go such a long way. The gospel to the poor is simple and straight forward: no gimmicks, no dressing Jesus up as someone else or depriving the cross of its full power. We can all contribute so much with the little we have and radically impact whole communities in poverty. There is one central gift He came to bring: life and love to all, and any way that we can release this brings joy to His heart.

Any way that we can give love brings joy to the heart of God

It is true that giving to the poor has its own dilemmas and issues; but despite all the difficulties and struggles, the heart of God is the same – give, provide for and help – regardless of how well it is received or whether people turn to God. We are always to be in this place with arms extended and open, as much as we are able. There is a purity in this: a purity in simplicity and the lack of required response or reciprocation on the part of those who receive from us. To give freely, like the purity of the gospel – we want people to know God for their own sake, with no strings attached; we are not concerned whether they join *our* churches or follow *our* stream or culture, but simply that the gift of life would wrap around their hearts and transform them heavenwards.

There is a power in the purity of simple giving

A key question I think we need to ask is: *does God respond to need?* Jesus appears to teach us that responding to need is good – because *how we treat others is how we treat Him* (ref. above). Jesus taught us in simplicity to *give to him who asks of you* (Mt.5:42). If we have the ability to help the poor before us and they ask of our help, yet we suppress the compassion of God, how can the love of God abide in us? (1 Jn.3:17-18). If we do not help He will not hear our prayers; conversely, if we help them and look after them He will look after us (Pr.21:13, 11:24-25). His inference is – if we do not respond to this need, we have missed the heart of God. We are indebted in one thing only – to love. If we have the power to give today, God knows we can and in many cases we ought (Pr.3:28). This pure heart to look after the poor, the orphans and the widow, treating them as our own; this is pure religion in the eyes of God – because it is His heart (Jam.1:27). To me this sounds like *the true spirit of fathering* – everyone is important, everyone's needs should be met, we want the whole community to be well looked after and none to lack.

The one obvious legitimate exception to our giving to the poor is where God has clearly directed our resources elsewhere (e.g. for the purposes of expanding the kingdom). I believe we can make a case for possessions above and beyond our need, but only for our work – to provide for our families and for others, and for the advancement of the kingdom of God. I always feel so challenged when revisiting this as I have always had my needs met with ease.

The challenge of Jesus in Luke 12 was clear and strong; I believe His intention is simply to keep our hearts uncorrupted and to prevent us from becoming attached to this world. He warned at other times of the folly of trusting in riches – they will distract us from the kingdom. We can only serve one master and godliness with contentment is great gain (Lk.16:13, Mk.10:23-25, 1 Tim.6:6).

"Only aim at and strive for and seek His kingdom, and all these things shall be supplied to you also... Sell what you possess and give donations to the poor; provide yourselves with purses and handbags that do not grow old, an unfailing and inexhaustible treasure in the heavens..."

Lk.12:31, 33

- Only seek the kingdom -

- Jesus

Even John the Baptist taught - let him who has two coats give one away: i.e. let all those in need be provided for out of our abundance before we take it to ourselves... this is one of the only things we are aware of that John taught, but was potentially key in reforming the peoples' understanding about how to treat each other properly - true repentance and cultural change in preparation for the coming of Jesus. It seems fair that we take this as a principle of following Jesus, we cannot get away from this *simply having enough and then giving the rest we have away.* (How challenged I feel writing this!!!)

The truth is: He has made us free so that we can live from the overflow of our hearts; this is why He loves us giving generously and liberally. This long standing principle of giving from *a willing heart* is paramount in the eyes of God (Ex.35:5). He promises to be gracious in provision so that we may have more than enough in order that we can give:

"[Remember] this: he who sows sparingly and grudgingly will also reap sparingly and grudgingly, and he who sows generously will also reap generously with blessings. Let each one [give] as he had made up his own mind and purposed in his heart, not reluctantly or sorrowfully or under compulsion, for God loves a cheerful giver [whose heart is in his giving]. And God is able to make all grace come to you in abundance, so that you may always and under all circumstances and whatever the need be self-sufficient. ...Thus you will be enriched in all things and in every way, so that you can be generous, and [your generosity as it is] administered by us will bring forth thanksgiving to God"

2 Cor.9:6-8, 11*

We are free to give from the overflow of our hearts

There are a few further principles that apply to our giving: firstly for *equality within the kingdom* – that all needs be met, secondly that we should give according to our ability (2 Cor.8:12-15), and thirdly that we should be content with food, clothing and shelter (1 Tim.6:8-10). Beyond our basic needs, all we own is Christ's, and we as faithful stewards are to wisely invest our resources for the good of the many.

Let there be equality

Let all needs be met

If we consider how Jesus values people and how He regards the least so highly – He encourages us to associate with the poor, the downtrodden, the forgottens of society. If we combine this with His teachings on service, the call is not only to associate with the outcasts, *but put them first*, even become their servants! His principles of leadership call us to become a *servant to all* and to *lead by example,* such is the highest form in the kingdom of heaven (Mk.10:44). (There is of course one caveat to this – we must not neglect our other duties before the Lord; in the case of the early apostles – their primary service was to share the Word of God! Acts 6:4). We see that to Jesus, the greatest in the kingdom invests their life in those considered insignificant in the world's eyes, but precious to God: Not only precious, but *priceless* (all people truly are, and we are too used to systematically devaluing things in society by assigning an economic price…). In our day we sense a heightened awareness of desire to make our lives significant, to make a difference. In the eyes of God, laying down our lives for the least is among the most significant of things we can do. Anyone who sees themselves above associating with the lowly and engaging in service by humble tasks has become proud. Everyone is worthy of our time and perhaps this is one of the greatest challenges of all!

Fight for Justice.

Uphold right from wrong.

Protect the weak.

Defend the vulnerable.

Justice is a fundamental expression of love

Injustice requires confrontation

Righteous anger is love raging against evil

Provoked by the suffering of our neighbour

Impassioned for uncompromised justice

How can we awaken both conscience and consciousness?

Especially toward the reality of injustice in the world?

The solidarity of the brotherhood

The humanity of vulnerability

The open hearted way of honesty

We are in this together

What about God directing us in our giving? The options for helping people are endless in a world so in need with global travel and communication freely accessible. Opportunities may be ubiquitous, but our resources are still so limited: we have a little time, perhaps a little monetary resource and a few skills we may be able to utilize to help. No matter what our geographical, cultural and economic context in this world, we are surrounded by the poor. It does seem therefore the practical thing to do – to get specific direction from the Lord as to where we can be most effective. It would be easy, when feeling the very compassion of God and seeing the need, to feel overwhelmed by the size of the task – especially when some poor folks do not want help. I'm not sure anyone has the answers for this. We know that at times the burden of lost souls can feel equally overwhelming and no doubt God knows how we feel. We have found that in casting our cares upon Him, we can somehow remain at rest in the midst of it all. All I really know is, it is perfectly natural to have the poor in our remembrance (Gal.2:10), to consider them one of our primary focuses for aid, and to love on the people who are most in need and receptive. Jesus spoke of the poor as always being with us, whilst affirming our freedom to give to them whenever we wish (Mk.14:7). Many folks in our generation have been inspired by the principle the Bakers (Iris Ministries) have pioneered: *stopping for the one* – the one in front of us, to do what we can today and leave the rest in the arms of God, this is certainly a pragmatic viewpoint and a good place to start!

Let us learn to value every little thing that people give

Never taking anything for granted

Do we value peoples' time and heart enough?

One of the greatest victories of the kingdom of God is the liberation of the heart and spirit through communion with God – regardless of the trials of the body. The life of the spirit is the true life, valuable above all that the world can offer. Is it any wonder that such a victory triumphs for the poor and shouts louder than all the joys of the rich? Is it any wonder that God would choose such a way to liberate man – that elevates those who have nothing – having in Him more than all the world could ever offer? Such is a grace worthy of the greatest God, such is a plan of such great glory! We are truly in awe of the wisdom of God!

- The kingdom of God is worth more
than all the riches of this life -

The Macedonians

"We want to tell you further, brethren, about the grace of God which has been evident in the churches of Macedonia; For in the midst of an ordeal of severe tribulation, their abundance of joy and their depth of poverty have overflowed in wealth of lavish generosity on their part. For, as I can bear witness according to their ability, yes, and beyond their ability; and voluntarily, begging us most insistently for the favour and the fellowship of contributing in this ministration for the saints in Jerusalem."

2 Cor.8:1-4

It is rare for one to give all that they have. It is especially rare for a company of people to attempt to give themselves into poverty for the sake of others. A heart of love can willingly give itself into suffering, poverty – even attempt to give beyond one's ability and such the Macedonians did. There is the instruction of God to give, and then there is the overflow of our own hearts! We see here that love chooses sacrifice: *for the joy set before us enduring the cross* (Heb.12:2), giving ourselves into poverty for love, finding even the lowest places in order to lift others up (Phil.2:5-8). Such is the Spirit of Christ and what a glorious example! No doubt the Lord gave them every grace to sustain them in their time of need.

"...He was so very rich, yet for your sakes He became poor, in order that by His poverty you might become enriched."

2 Cor.8:9

Extravagance

What is it about extravagance that is so powerful? The message is so clear, unchallengeable, cannot be doubted. When we choose to love extravagantly – to act in an unprecedented way; in a heartfelt manner that clearly cost us a lot, *people are left hanging* – walls come crumbling down. The intent of love is so clear in our extravagance. Extreme generosity guarantees that the message is delivered!

– The Heart –

The kingdom of God is within you

God has given us a Spirit of love: His Spirit in our hearts

Lk.17:21, 2 Tim.1:7, 2 Cor.1:22, Rom.14:17

The Battle of Our Lives

The greatest battle we will ever face is the one over our own hearts and minds. This is the battle of holiness. The classic perspective taken on spiritual warfare in the last few decades has focused on the battles of angels and demons in the heavens; dealt with by *discernment and declarations*, always focused on the enemy without. Whilst this spiritual reality certainly exists, the greatest fight will always be *the battle of our souls* and this is most often how spiritual warfare manifests tangibly. Once our hearts are set unchangeably on the face of God, these devils have no power to tempt us away. Seeing the true nature of spiritual warfare can be extremely beneficial in diffusing an unhelpful focus on our enemies and neglecting our simple responsibility as the custodian of our own heart before God.

"Keep and guard your heart with all vigilance and above all that you guard, for out of it flow the springs of life."

Pr.4:23

"He who believes in me as the scripture has said, from his innermost being shall flow [continuously] springs and rivers of living water."

Jn.7:38*

"Does a fountain send forth [simultaneously] from the same opening fresh water and bitter?"

Jam.3:13

One of the clearest principles we find in the teachings of Jesus is: *true life is a matter of the heart and spirit.* He taught us that *the flesh profits nothing* and the Spirit gives life (Jn.6:63), and that *the kingdom is within us* (Lk.17:21). *"God is a spirit and those who worship Him must worship Him in spirit and in truth,"* the Father is seeking true worshippers! (Jn.4:23-24). When Jesus reinterprets the teachings of the Jews, He clarifies the original intention and purposes of them – pointing to *the heart.* It is quite profound that Jesus taught a new way which overturns the separatist interpretations of the law. Jesus was exceptionally good at getting to the heart of the matter, and may we learn to be also. We can draw the conclusion that one of the primary reasons we may not experience the life of the kingdom is that we are not living the life of the spirit! If we sow to the spirit we will reap life!

"And I will give them a heart to know Me"

Jer.24:7

Those who walk most closely with God

will become the most loving people on earth.

The Heart of Christ

In seeking God for His abiding presence, we have sought to diffuse the mystique surrounding the realisation of His *permanent* presence. God has revealed to us the way to come into continual permanent tangible communion with the Lord: through the union of our hearts with His. When a heart to heart connection is established between us and heaven, His presence manifests – this is the oneness of God (and sometimes this is as simple as turning our attention heavenwards). The best way that I have heard this experience described was through the visions of Paul Keith Davies, as detailed in *Thrones of Our Soul*. True *"He who is joined to the Lord is one spirit with Him"* (1 Cor 6:17) – already, *and* we have free access to His presence by faith and through the blood of Christ (Eph.3:12). Nonetheless, our understanding of this dynamic confirms our experiences and explains *how* the Lord is intending to lead us into the fulfilment of His promise: *to abide with us tangibly.*

Many have observed how the scriptural analogy of *fruit* teaches us about the way that we are to become fruitful: *to simply receive the Holy Spirit and the Word*, to simply drink of the water of life – for we know a tree does not try to bear fruit, bearing fruit is part of its nature, it cannot help it. When we live in an atmosphere of the Spirit of God, at some point love will explode into the forefront of our lives. The Spirit of God will reveal His love to us, remaining with us as a tangible presence and we will learn to love the way He does. *"He* who walks [as a companion] with wise men is wise..." (Prov.13:20) In the same way, he who walks with lovers will become one. It is just as the Lord said – "You will know them by their fruits" (Mt.7:15-20) and those who walk most closely with God will become the most loving people on earth.

"...Ever be filled and stimulated with the Spirit" (Eph.5:18) – this is a present and continuous experience.

We could also say, since "God is love" (1 Jn.4:8) and "...the love of Christ controls and urges and impels us" (2 Cor.5:14):

Ever be filled and stimulated with love.

So many facets of good character naturally reside in a loving heart: all of the fruits of the Spirit can be born of love (Gal.5:22-23). When love overflows from the heart we start to behave in all the ways that resemble godliness: honouring, respectful etc... By way of example, if we are choosing to love someone, we will attempt to be as patient with them as possible: loves hopes all things, and in this heart wanting the best for them, we will never give up on them. When interacting with people, we will seek to be gentle and kind: these are the natural states of the loving heart. Our communication and sense of connection with people are guided largely by our body language, tone of voice, presence etc., often to a much greater degree than what we verbalise. Thank God He affects all these aspects so profoundly! When the Spirit of God is overflowing, people will feel deeply loved. We could examine all the traits of good character one by one to observe how love can act as their source; but once we see the principle it stands self evident. It is necessary therefore to simply be good custodians of our heart: its primary state and attitude, as we are encouraged in the timeless proverb:

"Keep and guard your heart with all vigilance and above all that you guard, for out of it flow the springs of life."

Prov.4:23

"To the pure all things are pure"

Titus 1:15

The love of God purifies the heart

1 Pet.1:22

"By mercy and love, truth and fidelity, iniquity is purged out of the heart, and by the reverent worshipful fear of the Lord men depart from and avoid evil."

Pr.16:6*

"As he thinks in his heart, so is he"

Pr.23:7

"He who has a glad heart has a continual feast"

Pr.15:15

"Whoever trusts in the Lord, happy is he"

Pr.16:20, NKJV

The seat of our meditations determines the state of our hearts, as Jesus also taught, *"for where your treasure is, there will your heart be also"* (Lk.12:34). When our hearts become so attached to the heavenly, we lose interest in the earthly; our selfish motivations have died and from this place our only motivation is to do what He is asking for His sake.

The wisdom of heaven is full of compassion

Jam.3:16-17

We have the mind and Spirit of Christ in us. We have the thoughts and feelings of His heart (1 Cor.2:16). We have His peace, the very peace He walked in (Jn.14:27). We are to put on Christ – His very nature, to imitate Him, to walk as He did (1 Cor.11:1, 15:49, Eph.4:24). Without contention, our hearts are to become just as His: to beat for what His beats for, to be aware of His feelings and thoughts, to see His plans. The words of our mouths are a sure sign of the true state of our hearts (Mt.12:24). When the words of Christ abundantly flow from our hearts, God will grant His Spirit without measure (Jn.3:24). When we look at the connection between heart and love, we are talking about God rewiring us so that our natural motivations come into accord with His heart. Perhaps then it is unsurprising that we can find ourselves in a place where His love compels, even controls us – where we are led, carried, even possessed by His heart – overwhelming our ability to resist, overwhelming any residual selfish inclination – love is the greatest motivator after all. Many believers have talked of various experiences they have had: where for a moment they were so compelled it was as if God had taken over completely, is this what Paul was talking about?

The love of Christ compels and controls us

(2 Cor.5:14)

The Spirit of love lives in our hearts. He is fearless. He is disciplined. Jesus was *moved by compassion*, but not just in a moment, He lived from this place. Will we continue to be moved by compassion even when it becomes really costly?

Moved

> And moved...

> > *And moved...*

> > > **Moved**

> > > **By Compassion**

When people become our treasure the battle is won. There is a profound awakening that comes when we see: *people really are the only thing that matters,* love recognises this and will not back down from it. Furthermore, Love will enable us to continually pay the highest price for people, and without it we may fail them, or even fall short of revealing the full strength of God's heart to them.

You think you've seen militant?

Wait until you meet love face to face.

- fire in His eyes

Hearts Wide Open

"Our mouth is wide open to you, Corinthians (we are hiding nothing, keeping nothing back), and our heart is expanded wide [for you]! There is no lack of room for you [in our hearts], but you lack room in your own affections [for us]... open wide your hearts also [to us]... I do not say this to reproach or condemn [you], for I have said before that you are [nested] in our hearts, [and you will remain there] together [with us], whether we live or die."

2 Cor.6:11, 12, 13, 7:3

As our love grows, our hearts expand. There is a place that we can grow into, from which we want to welcome everyone with open arms. God can open our hearts wide enough for every person that we ever meet. A free heart is an open heart: there is a willingness to share life and soul. Paul urges the Corinthians to open wide their hearts, to pull down the walls! He tells the Philippians how he carries them in his heart (Phil.1:7): they are in his thoughts and prayers day and night; his concern is for their all round prosperity and he can never forget. In his letters he left them in little doubt as to his affections for them.

Jesus considered that He had opened Himself up to His disciples:

"Have I been with you all this time and do you not know me yet?"

Jn.14:9

I imagine this is almost a puzzlement to Jesus – *really?! I've been revealing The Father to you all this time and you still don't recognise Him? How can this be possible?!*

Jesus was a direct channel for the Father's love into the lives of others, we can become this channel in the same way (Jn.15:9, 12); when we walk as He did, we will love each other in the way that He loves us.

We may even find ourselves saying the same things - *Have I been with you so long – do you not see The Father?!*

Not only this, but His lovingkindness draws us to Him (Jer.31:3, Rom.2:4). As we become His channel of love to others, they will be attracted to us – we should not underestimate the power of this!

An open heart carries a willingness to be vulnerable if ever it will help someone else. It is a way of serving others and loving them – by laying ourselves bare and inviting them in to truly know us. People feel valued when we invest trust in them. The fullness of love makes us so secure that we can open up to anyone – and we know that if we get burned, His love will cover us, heal us, make us new and fresh again. It may take some time, but we can fully trust that His love is available to us as much as we need it in the midst of relational hardships. We cannot find a reason not to open up if we are done with maintaining facades and keeping up appearances – if we have nothing to prove anymore, no reputation to protect and we wish only to help others we can freely open wide our hearts. I am not suggesting of course that we knowingly put ourselves in situations where we are continually hurt by people, wisdom should always prevail. Nonetheless, the value of honesty and the desire for deeper connections will often draw us to open our hearts: it is better that we are real with each other, it is even better that people are aware of our weaknesses. We can best support one another when everything is out in the light. By opening our hearts it is an invitation to others to open theirs and by so doing we are leading the way into deeper relationship.

Love displaces fear

He is releasing the atmosphere of love

in which fear cannot hold together

Anxiety cannot exist when we know we are loved

Most of our soul issues are rooted in fear, often even our pride. The battle of *trust versus fear* appears to be the greatest fight we face. Love is the most comprehensive antidote. Furthermore, we have arrived at an understanding of the inherent interconnections between faith, love and trust. Faith and trust can be born from love and there is a place where love has been expressed to the degree that *it can no longer be doubted.* Many of us have experienced this in our personal relationship with the Lord, *I know that I am loved and literally nothing can change that.* This rock of love in our lives cannot be damaged or removed; we are forever secure in the goodness of God. All of our anxieties pale away in the heat of pure love. They will only return if we open the door by entertaining doubt, and this becomes increasingly difficult to do, (in one sense, anxiety *is doubting love*). We too can love others with a strength that displaces doubts and fears – to the point where *our commitment to love each other as best as we can is firmly established.* As we release love into people's lives, it will banish fear from them, *the two cannot coexist.* Imagine how radically changed people will be if a whole community gathers around them smothering them in love?!

- He paints love all over the walls of my heart -

Wholeness

Love released in a moment, *a glimpse of being completely loved,* that feeling of being *so loved that nothing else matters*. The security of *being loved in eternity,* the wonder that God planned *who we are.* At times we feel free to do anything in the power of God. How beautiful are these treasured moments – and furthermore we experience these delights as much in the place of romance with God as we do in the love of the Father!

The love of God is the healing force that affirms our identity, validity, security. We are empowered to face the twists and turns of life with the bold stance – *honestly, what are we afraid of?* It is the antidote to all our worries. It is the strength to endure all our troubles (for the joy set before us: joy born of love), It is the answer to so many questions...

God is love: *He cannot help it.* This is how He is wired! And of course this does not make His actions purely mechanical – He still enjoys and chooses so willingly to continue loving and being love. We are destined to live from identity, and in a sense this is what *abiding* is all about, we act like the ones we are following and we become that which we focus on (1 Jn.3:9-10).

– God is love –

One of the key gifts God has given me is a profound sense of wholeness. I have been so blessed through the gift of two very loving parents, who have not only been great parents to me, but genuine deep friends. I have never been in a position to doubt their love for me and for this I am truly grateful. Nonetheless, as a fourteen year old boy I faced the identity crisis and found myself deeply depressed for a time. In the midst of a place of self-loathing, darkness and the occasional thought to end it all, I came to realise that only God could rescue me. It is incredible to me: when we simply turn to Him with our struggles, how readily and quickly He delivers us (Lk.18:7). He spoke to me very clearly one day, seemingly out of the blue to this effect (I'm paraphrasing) –

I want you to be who I have created you to be. If you try to be someone else, you will fail to do this, and you will fail to be the person I have created you to be. The best thing you can do is be yourself. I have made you well.

Sometimes when God speaks it is like a harpoon to the heart. He writes His words on our hearts so strongly that they become part of us, and in this moment He settled the identity issue in me, breaking the darkness off me once for all in this area. Hindsight clarified the full effect of what the Lord had done through this – I was apparently one of the most secure teenagers in my identity from this point on. Such can be the effect of one word from God! To this day, people still testify how the security and freedom He has placed in me is such a blessing to them to see, I cannot express how grateful I am to Him for dealing with this so early on. I am confident that many of God's children have experienced this in their early years, for He is a God and Father so eager to bless His children with good gifts (Jam.1:17).

One word from God can change the course of our lives forever

God speaks words into our lives with such creative power that they literally form who we are

There has been a great deal of focus on inner healing in the past few decades. People frequently go for long weekends of ministry, prayer and teaching on the quest for wholeness. Frequently new techniques and ideas spring up, and for some folks they are yet to find their relief; they have tried it all and endured no end of prayer sessions in the hope of finding wholeness in their hearts. Without a doubt, God has done incredible things through the inner healing movement and many have found their freedom through it. (The best thing we can do with any issue is to get to the root of it and deal with it permanently...) How can we guide those who are still searching for wholeness? Clearly every case is specific, and there is no clear formula but to seek God for answers and breakthrough. What we have come to understand however, is that absent the formation of a deep personal relationship with God from which life flows out, we may not find the wholeness we seek. One thing I can say for sure is that God does deal with things in a permanent way, there are issues I simply don't battle with anymore – He can do a lasting work – *once for all!*

His transformation of us is as much into the positive – the very nature of Christ, as it is out of insecurities, which is why I believe we can become people who always love. We have so often focused on issues we are seeking to wrestle free from, but the people who appear to be most whole have become most transfixed on Him. As with the battle of overcoming sin, we need to be filled with the Holy Spirit and the Word – every void needs to be filled with the substance of light. When we become people full of the Word, we build a solid light foundation, a platform for heavens abode in our lives. The seeds of darkness cannot take root in soil that is full of the goodness and truth of God. We must become full of His Truth!

Absent an encounter with the love of God, there are aspects of our nature nothing else will fix. Personally speaking, I have found my abiding wholeness in knowing Him, in spending quality time with Him one on one – *there is no substitute for spending time in the presence of the Lord*, no substitute for hearing His voice personally and bathing in His love. So often we find that coming to the source – coming to the solution, fixes so many problems without having to tackle them head on. We fix the eyes of our hearts on His and our soul troubles melt away. Can it be this simple? There is a great chorus of testimony resounding through the world today which validates the power in this simple principle. Since so many people are now living this out, could it work for everyone?

Love rewrites the book of destiny before our eyes

Our expectations are forever hijacked by grace when love takes over

We begin to expect so much from God with little effort from ourselves

We have become so aware of His desire for us.

The years of spiritual striving are gone forever.

He loved me into believing His grace

Now I feel His heart beating every time I breathe

What could eclipse this?

Love silences all our insecurities.

He has become our absolute security

Knowing We Are Loved

There is something so deeply reassuring to know, whatever happens, *You still love me*; it is like Jesus said, *"no one can take from you your joy* (Jn.16:22),"
"...neither death nor life, nor angels, nor principalities, nor things impending, and threatening nor things to come, nor powers, nor height, nor depth, nor anything else in all creation will be able to separate us from the love of God (Rom.8:37-38)." When we know this with deep certainty in our hearts, there is little in life that can truly unsettle us.

Whatever happens, You still love me

I was meditating one day on 1 Cor.13... The phrase *"Love believes all things"* was highlighted to my spirit by the Lord, *"I believe in you"* He said. Immediately the thought comes to mind – but how? You know how much of a failure I am, You know all my mistakes and sins, surely You of all people know whether I will succeed and do not invest this *faith in me?* Is it not that I am supposed to lose all faith in the earthly, in myself and my own abilities? Surely power is found in our only trusting in God and yielding all we have to Him? He wasn't about to answer my theological objections.

God believes in you.

He knows you can.

After all, *He is GOD.*

And He is with you!

Over time He brought clarity to this gift of confidence He was giving me. Our earthly fathers believe in us, not just because they know our abilities, but they also know that they can help us – and they absolutely intend on doing so. God is the one who is most able to help us and desires to, which is not to say that He will make life easy at all; only that He intends to enable us to fulfil His plans for our lives, and let us not forget for a second:

HE IS GOD ALMIGHTY.

The Life Changing Power of a Love Encounter

In interviewing just half a dozen people about their experiences in God for a documentary, we quickly discovered a profound truth resounding throughout all their testimonies. In answer to a question phrased similarly to the following one – *have you had any key turning points, moments or experiences in your life that have profoundly changed your course?* The answer would come back straight away, without any prompt and often in an awakened state of excitement – Yes! *God showed me He loved me.* In each case they would expound on the details of the experience, but the result was nearly always exactly the same: God showed me in a real tangible way His deep love for me, and I have never been the same again – above all other experiences: supernatural, profound and mystical, peoples first response was always about love directly revealed.

Another characteristic I have noticed about love is the apparent lasting quality – the residing affects when people encounter it. This is confirmed through conversations with a variety of people about their experiences; we have found that when love is present, there seems to be the greatest potential for lasting transformative experiences.

– A Covenant Beyond Our Dreams –

Uniting all the world to Christ again.

Life for all men

Rom.5:18

It may help to keep in mind, that a true covenant is a lifelong unbreakable agreement, historically cut in blood – the deepest union which can be created between men, binding us together with the strength and commitment of family evermore.

An understanding of covenant is essential both as a basis for understanding history and the profound depths of biblical truths. The breaking of covenant is the most serious of failures. God will not break covenant with us, He will not relent (Ps.89:33-34, Jer.30:20-21).

All Things Are Possible

If it isn't obvious already, I believe that the visions God has given us can be fulfilled *now*, here on earth (Lk.1:37, etc.) – *all things are possible!* Why give us such a promise if He didn't intend to do *all things that we can dream of for His glory?!*

"For with God nothing is ever impossible and no word from God shall be without power or impossible of fulfilment."

Lk.1:37

We have often taken the view that much of what God has established in the Great Covenant will only be fulfilled at the end time when heaven becomes fully manifest. He is in the process of unlocking many great truths and experiences and showing us just how much He wants to do *now*, and in all fairness, it is mind-blowing.

God does not speak to us without reason and purpose. I've learned over many years that when He is drawing my attention to a situation, it is so often an indicator – of His intention to speak into it *now*, to move, to leave His mark on it. In conversation, He opens up a world of incredible dreams so far beyond us; but how could we expect anything less from a God who is infinitely greater than our comprehension, our desires, our visions (Eph.3:20). If we have a heart for something glorious, His is always greater and He is the source of that heart – of all that we have learned to love and value.

God speaks to us : in hopes & dreams

There can be a difficult tension that we live with: we see the incredible potential and heart of God, this awakens our very passions for Him to fulfil these visions, and yet in faith and patience we are waiting for the fulfilment (Heb.6:12). This is especially poignant when there is no earthly sign or precedent for the vision that we hope for. If the reality of our experience does not soon match up with the gift of God, it is easy to become discouraged and doubt. The Lord is so persistent and steadfast. He continues to insist that we trust Him to do everything that He has promised us, and after all – it will eventually come by our faith and patience, not our abandoning hope! In our common experience, we find patience the hardest part. Nonetheless, there is a compelling dynamic that exists in the love of God which causes our hope to become hard wired, we cannot lose it! We simply trust and believe! Our prayer is for the Lord to grant us every strength to persist and rest in His patience. Our hope is further empowered by knowing that in Christ all He has promised us will eventually be fulfilled *somewhere* on the earth – wherever there is a covenant promise God will accomplish it in a people before the end of time!

A company of God's people somewhere in the earth

will see the fulfilment of all God's promises!

Reformation in Progress

In the last half dozen years the Holy Spirit has been particularly drawing us in to explore the heart of God and re-examine our theology. As a consequence of this, we see a great abundance of fruit, which is most clearly seen in an abundance of new found freedom. There are a number of key points we have discovered which stand out – that we can all experience communion with God freely, that we all have a significant calling in God, that God has opened the depths of the Spirit to us all and that He deeply, deeply love us. We thank God dearly for that which He is establishing in our generation!

Some of the great truths that are being restored are proving exceptionally effective at building a foundation of faith for the revealing of the kingdom of God in our generation. For example, the reality of *the kingdom of heaven is at hand* – i.e. that heaven is as close as our breath, if only we'll believe – is becoming mainstream doctrine. An understanding of the full gospel has dawned within the multitude – that the salvation *(sozo)* gift we are offered means that we are not only saved from our sins, but that in Christ we are healed, delivered from darkness and set at peace, evermore. A renewed focus on the completeness of the work of Christ, and the call to put our full trust in Him alone is also being established. The consequence of this is a greater reliance on the Holy Spirit and the end of the *methods and formula's* taught for the previous few decades ('7 steps to the glory' or whatever), which so often set up new 'charismatic laws' for entering 'the deep things of the spirit' over simply believing clear biblical truths (eg. Eph.3:12). In a sense, the Holy Spirit has undone our reliance on *what we think we already know about Him,* re-established an acceptance of the unknown and a degree of mystery, whilst removing our desire to have it all worked out or to rely on ourselves. *Let him who glories, glory in the Lord!* (2 Cor.10:17)

As often occurs when a company of people set out on a new pathway, there are a number of ideas that folks have begun to embrace which appear somewhat at odds with the full truth of God and His intentions –*the emphasis is slightly off the mark.* For example, some have elevated grace as an absolute truth, i.e. *'everything we believe about God must fit into our understanding of grace.'* It is clear though that God is truly *God,* and whilst He has extended His grace to us freely, it is not with the purpose that we are free to do simply as we please or to neglect the teachings of Jesus and His call of discipleship.

Some have also begun to teach a gospel which implies that the work of Christ is *so finished* that there is nothing left for us to do. *Any doctrine which allows us to miss the compassion of the present has not the love of God in it.* We cannot fail to recognise the difficulties we face as believers and the need in the world that surrounds us – and not be fully satisfied! To say the work of God is finished, without our hearts pining for the manifestation of the very glories He has bought for us is to *miss the heart of God.* How can any follower of Christ not long for the kingdom of God to come in the lives of all the people that we meet? It is not enough that Christ made heavenly possibilities available to us in this Great Covenant; *the love of God seeks their full manifestation here now!* Whilst standing eyes to heaven and calling on God for the coming of His kingdom; we cannot escape the *now and not yet,* the God who was and is and is to come, that in time all will be fulfilled, but *all is not yet here.* Knowing also, that in the present we have a significant role in bringing the fulfilment of these dear promises: in creating love stories, God stories, and to have such a strong compassion where heaven has not yet come!

Heavenly Expectations

As we stand on this Great Covenant we have with God, we now live by the spirit and we access this by faith. We live according to the law of the Spirit of *life*, which is *to obey the Holy Spirit*. It is otherwise spoken of as the *perfect law of liberty* (Jam.1:25, 2:8). We also know that in this Covenant there is no law against doing anything good: the actions of the Spirit – the fruits of the Spirit: there is no law against loving, being joyful, peaceful, being kind to one another, having extreme patience, the gentleness of the Spirit... At any time, if it is in our heart to be good to others, we are free to. Why is this important? We have established the notion that – walking rightly before God in the Great Covenant can only be done by the heart of God in us and by the power of the Spirit (2 Cor.3:5, Phil.2:13, Rom.8:2, 14). We know that we can ask for anything we need to do this, and we know that *in Him is all the love* that He wishes to pour out through us, we are therefore in a place of need – to simply say, Lord – *release Your heart and Your power*, and we know it is His will to give it.

My point here is simply, that this beautiful gift of eternal life in Christ is one to be experienced now; and that the tangible reality of it is His gift to us (the substance of which *will* transform others also). Spiritual realities all carry active substances – there is a substance of faith (Heb.11:1) and there is a substance of love. When someone testifies to experiencing immersion in the love and peace of God, they are encountering the bona fide spiritual substance of Heaven's love along with the integral physical reality it carries. We call this *God's presence*.

There is a direct link between faith and expectations – what we believe determines what we expect. The truth has been given to us in written form so that all can see what is available to us; that we might learn what to expect from God, and discern what is truly from Him. Knowing what is available to us empowers us to fight for it – for every justice in the earth. In this recent move of God He has been rewriting our expectations with an anticipation of heavenly realities on a daily basis. I believe it is completely fair to expect to tangibly experience the love of God regularly in powerful ways – we can live in this river permanently, so maybe the question is how? Or why do we not experience this already? When we hear of the great promises and gifts of this Great Covenant He has given us, we may find it more surprising that we don't experience the glory of union with Christ more frequently in greater power!

He has been rewiring our expectations

With an anticipation of heavenly realities on a daily basis

It is impossible to fulfil the call of God without experience. When we realise a thorough understanding of how the mind, heart and soul are wired; and combine this with the principle that the Great Covenant is one of the Spirit and not the letter, we arrive at a clear conclusion: living righteously can only be fulfilled through the direct impartation of heart, mind and spirit – the very Spirit and Heart of Christ – i.e. *the blueprint for encounters with God*. Anyone who now denies, or attempts to denigrate the experience of God in the Great Covenant, *has not understood the Great Covenant or God's heart.* Experience is and will be the key to the fulfilment of right living and the manifestation of Jesus – *and* He has already given us the keys to enter this world of spiritual experience – i.e. *the Word* and *faith* – we can simply ask Him. However, we are still dependent on Him opening it up to us (as always).

This truth clearly does not detract from the imperative to *do what is right – obedience to God regardless of whether we feel like it*; we are simply acknowledging that we need His input and His power at all times, and so we act in faith and take risks in those moments when we do not yet see clearly. Furthermore, how often does He meet us in power upon our decision to obey and *step out!?*

The reason for establishing the crucial importance of our experience, is to clarify that He wants to bring us into a place where *obedience is the full joy of our hearts* (Heb.1:9), our feelings come into line and our faith steps will result in the tangible release of His power.

I am conscious a point of clarity may be beneficial here. I do not believe we should give credence to the flawed dichotomy of *'experience versus word'* that often follows on from discussion of this subject. So many theological debates are founded on a false notion of *'either or'* when in truth we need both, the pertinent question is *which now?* And for the record, while we're on the subject, *hearing the word is an experience*, and one which obedience should always follow. Ultimately, Jesus put it best when He said: *"the words that I have been speaking to you are spirit"* (Jn.6:63).

- This Great Covenant is a blueprint for encounters with God -

God frequently works in our lives when we are not tangibly aware of it (though we are becoming more aware as time proceeds). When we consider the baptism of the Spirit, this is a literal receiving of the person of the Holy

Spirit into our bodies, hearts and spirits; with this in mind, it seems bizarre that we have accepted a notion of *'receiving the Spirit'* without an experience – consider the absurdity of receiving someone into your life without any sign or change or direct impact – not to mention God Himself!!!

If we think about the notion of *God* moving and working... is it possible that God can work in the earth without massively impacting people and leaving clear signs along the way? Of course I am not suggesting that we seek after the signs, but that the idea of God *moving* without significant and tangible changes appearing down the line and great in abundance is absurd! Especially when He seems so willing to reveal Himself tangibly to those who diligently seek Him (Heb.11:6) again and again. This is the testimony of the generations!

Not a generation goes by without a people alive on the earth who are aware of God's heart and intentions

(Amos.3:7)

We have an absolutely solid foundation for expecting the greatest richness of life in this Covenant. The presence of God is a gateway to experiencing Him. In His presence is fullness of joy and at His right hand are pleasures forevermore (Ps.16:11). Let us not forget David experienced this before Christ came! Jesus came that we might have *fullness of life!* (John 10:10, Col.2:10) If God lives in us, *how can we not have fullness of life? (Jesus teachings clearly show this full life is found predominantly in the spirit).* In response, we are left with a number of questions – Do we believe it? Do we expect it? Why have we not been experiencing this full life to date? And what can we do about it?

He came that we might have fullness of life

"He who did not withhold or spare [even] His own Son but gave Him up for us all, will He not also with Him freely and graciously give us all [other] things?"

Rom.8:32

When we consider the issues at the heart of why moves of God come and go; there are a number of key principles that resound from both scripture and history. To some degree, we are able to distinguish the characteristics of those who experienced the blessings of the Promised Land from those who did not. People of faith, who live in deep prayer; who take risks and live in absolute consecration and holiness; those who live as citizens of heaven as before the very throne of God (2 Cor.2:17) – these very sons of the kingdom saw their worlds turned upside down. They are like those men of old *of whom the world was not worthy* (Heb.11:38).

In almost every case of revival that we are aware of in history, the cost was ever so high – God would not allow compromise or devotion to other things. I know not of any folks, who have sought God deeply and diligently, who have not come to experience the liberties and communion with Him that their heart's desired. Without exception they all do! Perhaps we hoped that the kingdom of God would come, both in our hearts and around us, free of the pursuit and high cost, free of such a deep consecration, and without coming to really know God personally?

There are times when God has responded to my prayers only when I have become desperate enough to pursue Him *until* He released that very thing for which I was seeking Him. There are times when He will not allow it to be easy for us. His response may not be quick for our own sake, in order that we would value what we receive from Him, and because He is seeking our full attention and our time. This dynamic is not too dissimilar from the parable of the unjust judge in terms of how we are encouraged to seek Him in persistence (Lk.18:1-8, but even this reference notes His desire to *deliver us speedily!*) My faith in God's willingness and ability to bring us into this full life is not the least bit deterred by the testimony of those whom have not yet experienced the deep liberties of the Spirit. Furthermore, at no point does He say that this full life will come without suffering. The early disciples rejoiced in the sufferings of Christ, seeing the glory that they are! Let us not forget this – the sufferings of this present time *are not worthy of being compared* with the glory that shall follow, and that to suffer for Him is a highest honour (Acts 5:41, Heb.11:26, 2 Cor.12:10).

"Indeed all who delight in piety and are determined to live a devoted and godly life in Christ Jesus will meet with persecution."

2 Tim.3:12*

"...For I consider that the sufferings of this present time are not worth being compared with the glory that is about to be revealed to us and in us..."

Rom.8:18*

"For our light, momentary affliction is ever more and more abundantly preparing and producing and achieving for us an everlasting weight of glory, since we consider and look not to the things that are seen but to the things

that are unseen; for the things that are visible are temporal, but the things that are invisible are deathless and everlasting."

2 Cor.4:17-18*

- Overtaken by the life of the spirit -

"Always carrying about in the body the liability and exposure to the same putting to death that the Lord Jesus suffered, so that the life of Jesus also may be shown forth by and in our bodies...

...Thus death is actively at work in us, but [it is in order that our] life [may be actively at work] in you."

2 Cor.4:10, 12*

Life, Death & Love

There is a principle regarding suffering active in the Great Covenant: that physical suffering and sacrifice can release spiritual power (1 Pet.3:18). Someone coined the well known phrase *'fire always comes upon sacrifice'* and our experiences seem to ring true! *"It is through many hardships and tribulations we must enter the kingdom of God"* (Acts 14:22). We also see here again – *love choosing to suffer* in order to bring life to others. For Paul this was a present and constant experience, and his letters are full of the evidence of such great suffering. The Captain of our salvation was made perfect through suffering (Heb.2:10) – leaving us an example (1 Pet.2:21); and we are to arm ourselves with the same mind – to suffer; we know that when the Spirit of glory rests on us we will be persecuted (1 Pet.4:14) – this is a blessing! There appears to be no case that can be made and no reason found for a Christian life absent suffering.

I find it curious then that some are so eager in these times to do away with our sharing in the fellowship of Christ's sufferings; especially when *both the Lord and the Apostles taught these principles so clearly* again and again. We can truly know Him more deeply in the midst of these sufferings, and such can even draw us together in fellowship with one another. If these sufferings are working for us *an eternal weight of glory*, why would any believer ever wish to embrace such a baseless theology?! Some have even abandoned fasting, which when discovered as the true gem it is, no one would ever consider living without it! I am not denying that these things can be difficult, but what of eternal vision? What of patient endurance? What of finding God in all things? The same Spirit that raised Jesus from the dead dwells in us

(Rom.8:11). How can this Spirit live in us and not bring life to us in the midst of *every* death?

"So since Christ suffered in the flesh for us, for you, arm yourselves with the same thought and purpose. For whoever has suffered in the flesh is done with sin, so that he can no longer spend the rest of his natural life living by his human appetites and desires, but [he lives] for what God wills."

1 Pet.4:1-2*

"...That what is mortal may be swallowed up by life."

2 Cor.5:4

A second and even greater principle of this Covenant is *the overtaking of the Spirit of God* as the new and living way. Our walking free of the old man, the desires of the flesh and our sinful nature is facilitated by the Holy Spirit taking over. He births the heart of Christ in us, and we are carried away by these new desires. He promises in this Great Covenant that *He* will write His laws on our hearts! (Jer.31:33) God so fills us with Himself that there is no room left for our old nature. We struggle to draw any substantive distinctions between the notions of being clothed with Christ – *the new man*, and the killing of the deeds of the flesh. The most effective focus for our efforts appears to be setting our gaze upon Him, rather than trying so strongly to put off the evil ways and desires – to empty them from our hearts. We lose sight of the 'old' and every temptation as Christ fills our view in every direction. True some will say, surely we only need believe that the old is already dead to experience full freedom from it? For sure people do experience this liberty at times purely by faith, but I am yet to see anyone walk this out consistently who has not also experienced the tangible impartation of Christ's nature in them and the continual filling of the Spirit (Eph.5:18).

"A new heart will I give you and a new spirit will I put within you, and I will take away the stony heart out of your flesh and give you a heart of flesh. And I will put my Spirit within you and cause you to walk in My Statutes, and you shall heed my ordinances and do them..."

Ez.36:26-27

The Promise of Overwhelming Glory

We have the strongest basis to hope for incredible things from the Lord; His Word includes many statements and promises which indicate life in the Great Covenant is to be full of the glory of God. In 2 Cor.3 Paul outlines a case whereby the Great Covenant is shown to be of much greater glory than the Jewish Covenant:

"For if the service that condemns had glory, how infinitely more abounding in splendour and glory must be the service that makes righteous! Indeed, in view of this fact, what once had splendour has come to have no splendour at all, because of the overwhelming glory that exceeds and excels it. For if that which was but passing and fading away came with splendour, how much more must that which remains and is permanent abide in glory and splendour!"

2 Cor.3:9-11

In light of this, surely we can take any of the glories of the Jewish Covenant and expect greater from the Lord? Can we not also expect the same in relation to peoples' experiences of God in the New Covenant? Paul uses the direct comparison of the shining face and life of Moses to make his point, but what if we were to consider other great ones from the Old Covenant? John the Baptist jump-started a movement of repentance in a generation in preparation for the coming of Jesus. Jesus even taught *the same principle* – that there was no one greater than John before him and that *the least in the kingdom of heaven is greater than he!* (Mt.11:11)

How can the New Covenant not be much more glorious than the Old?!

He who is least in the kingdom of heaven

is greater than the greatest from the Old Covenant

As if these possibilities in God weren't crazy enough already, the New Testament writings are littered with incredible experiences of believers who have *exactly the same Covenant with God as we do*, and God pledges not to have favourites. If we are to look specifically at *the presence of God* we see the same pattern as well. When God has made such outrageous glories available to us, the question of why we may not be experiencing them seems paramount...

"All the promises of God in Him are yes, and in Him amen, to the glory of God"
2 Cor.1:20

- In the light of the glory of the New Covenant
the Old Covenant will appear to have *no glory* -

What Moses experienced cannot compare
with what is available to us today in Christ

God pledged to Moses that His presence would go with him and that He would give him rest, this was also God's response to Moses prayer to *know Him* (Ex.33:13-19).

How can the presence of God not abide with us constantly?

Can we imagine fullness of life,
without the constant manifestation of His glorious presence?

We are destined to become the actual manifestation
of the abiding temple of God
Eph.2:22

How can this be intangible?

"Do you not know that Jesus Christ is in you..?"
2 Cor.13:5
The word here is a personal experiential knowledge.

Love chose to give us free access to Himself, without end (Eph.3:12).

A Concise List: The Unfathomable Riches of Christ

He has given us His Spirit that we might realise these gifts given to us (1 Cor.2:9-10, 12): fullness of Joy (Ps.16:11, Jn.15:11), fullness of life (Jn.10:10), a river of living water (Jn.7:38), great, wonderful, intense and everlasting love (Eph.2:4, Jer.31:3), fullness of love both revealed to us and alive in our hearts (1 Jn.4:12), overflowing hope, full of peace: at all times and in all ways (Rom.15:13, 2 Thes.3:16), grace beyond measure (1 Tim.1:14, Eph.2:7), the unending riches of Christ (Eph.3:8), in every respect you have been enriched, in full power... complete knowledge... lacking nothing: lacking no Christian grace! (1 Cor.1:5, 7), to ever be filled and stimulated with the Spirit: i.e. we always can be (Eph.5:18), strength for all things in Christ (Phil.4:11-13), God will liberally supply our every need (Phil.4:19), the exceeding greatness of His power revealed in us and our lives (2 Cor.4:7), transformation into His very own image from one degree of glory to another (2 Cor.3:18), He will even reveal precious treasures of wisdom (Col.2:3), He is working all things to our good (Rom.8:28), He will always leads us in triumph (2 Cor.2:14) to bear the image of the man of heaven (1 Cor.15:49) in companionship with Jesus Christ! (1 Cor.1:9).

!!!

Selah doesn't cover it!

A company of people will one day live in abiding spiritual life

- So *why not us? Why not now?*

How can we not be overjoyed,
when we see His promises again?

This Great Covenant is *bursting* with potential.

He is so much and so perfectly light, life and love that we cannot define them anymore outside of Him. He is the standard bearer, He is the example: He is light, life and love. He is the supreme example of these and since the most useful definition is an example and not an intangible theory... Jesus Himself said: He is the way and the truth and the life, and by defining Himself so He implies:

I am the greatest example of all of these. I will not simply take you to them, or show you what they are: I will be them to you and I will be them more than any other experience that you will have in your life, I will redefine them for you in me, by who I am.

- Light, Life & Love -

The greatest glory to God is His redemption in the midst of trouble. We have often invested our hopes in our lives following a new, clearly defined track of idealistic *perfection*; rather than recognising the beauty and triumph of redemption as a greater sign. God intervenes in the real – that which people can relate to – a life of glory overcoming hardships as it were. As romantic as a life of divine order could be; the stories of God's intervention in the midst of such human and frail circumstances genuinely seem to draw us in to God even more.

He is

Redemption

Keys to Fullness

"May He grant you out of the rich treasury of His glory to be strengthened and reinforced with mighty power in the inner man by the [Holy] Spirit [Himself indwelling your innermost being and personality].May Christ through your faith [actually] dwell (settle down, abide, make His permanent home) in your hearts! May you be rooted deep in love and founded securely on love. That you may have the power and be strong to apprehend and grasp with all the saints [God's devoted people, the experience of that love] what is the breadth and length and height and depth [of it]; [That you may really come to know [practically through experience for yourselves] the love of Christ, which far surpasses mere knowledge [without experience]; that you may be filled [through all your being] unto all the fullness of God [may have the richest measure of the divine Presence and become a body wholly filled and flooded with God Himself]!"

Eph.3:16-19

Where do we start?!

Paul prays for the tangible dwelling of Christ in our hearts; for us to have the deep and secure foundation that only *knowing love* brings; he prays that we might experience all of the dimensions of God's love and that we would be filled to all the fullness of God. In this dynamic prayer he has connected *love as the deep, secure foundation,* to *experiencing the greatest fullness of God*; he prayed that we would have the power to grasp the full extent of the love of God. This is the one place where *experiencing the fullness of God* is directly mentioned in scripture, and it is in the context of knowing His love.

Waves of His gracious power, pulling us higher into the love song

Woven into the fabric of this delicate existence

A thousand thoughts, a thousand words of His love for me

Planned for : in this harmony of all our hopeful memories

Create the dawn of our sublime : The glory of Christ in me

You are the fragrance

"...The fragrance of the knowledge of God: everywhere"
2 Cor.2:14

The atmosphere of love spills out everywhere we go

When we carry the fragrance of love day and night: they will see Jesus

God is love

God is love

God is love

God is love

Christ is the fulfilment of the law.

(Rom.10:4)

Love, Grace & Law

Jesus taught that the entirety of the Mosaic Law is fulfilled in these sayings:

"And He replied to him, You shall love the Lord Your God with all your heart and with all your soul and with all your mind. This is the great and first commandment. And a second is like it: You shall love your neighbour as you do yourself. These two commandments sum up and upon them depend all the Law and the Prophets."

Mt.22:37-40

"And he replied, you must love the Lord your God with all your heart and with all your soul and with all your strength and with all your mind; and your neighbour as yourself. And Jesus said to him, you have answered correctly;

do this, and you will live."

Lk.10:27-28

"The whole law is complied with in the one precept, you shall love your neighbour as you do yourself."

Gal.5:14

"Let me ask you this one question: Did you receive the Spirit as the result of obeying the law and doing its works, or was it by hearing and believing? Are you so foolish and so senseless and so silly? Having begun with the Spirit are you now reaching perfection [by dependence] on the flesh?"

Gal.3:2-3

"Love does no wrong to one's neighbour [it never hurts anybody]

Therefore love meets all the requirements and is the fulfilling of the law."

Rom.13:10

If this is true, why do we even discuss the law anymore in terms of how we are to live? Surely our overwhelming focus should be on simply *how to love?*

67

Surely the debate on grace versus law is over when love stands up? The point is not grace or law, it is love! *Love has always been the measuring stick for right living.* Even if we were to talk to folks who do not know Jesus about our sin and our need for God; is it not most profoundly revealed in the lack of love found in a heart that is distant from Him?

The meaning of the law is to lead us to Christ (Gal.3:24, 1 Tim.1:8-10), it reveals man's sinful, selfish nature – and shows our need for God and a Saviour (Rom.5-8). In love there is no sin (1 Jn.2:10) – no fault, no wrong, no error – *period,* walking in love will lead us into full obedience to God (1 Jn.4:12). Since all the law is fulfilled in our walking in love, we see that God's intention *has always been* that we would be a people abiding in love.

Love your neighbour *as you do yourself. Meaning:* love your neighbour in the same way that you love yourself, take as much care to ensure they are well looked after as you do for yourself. It is not – *love your neighbour if you have any time left over*, we are to *carry our neighbours in our very hearts.* We have only one duty left in life, though it is the ultimate call to love. If we are able to help anyone, we are obliged to! Obviously this is within the balance and limit of our resources and not neglecting our first calling to love on God and obey Him.

The Spirit loves freely

There is still much debate in Christian circles regarding law and grace – what does grace look like? What standard should we live by? Should we be rid of the law entirely? The traditionalists often accuse the libertarians of being too free, of having sloppy grace, and of disregarding the commands of God; whilst the libertarians accuse the traditionalists of being bound under law and religious, without having the freedom of the Spirit – both camps viewing the others' perspective as less spiritual. If we understand that the purpose of the law is to bring us to love and that by loving we walk right before God, I wonder how much we need debate the finer points of right and wrong? A law could never make us righteous because a law is not the Spirit of love; it is not the heart of God! Maybe the question we should always ask is – *is it love?*

When Jesus challenged the religious culture of the day, He struck at the elements which produced outcasts; He was derided as a friend of sinners and faced the same persecutions they did. In love His walk was bound to those society condemned. His rebukes to the religious centred on their *missing the entire point: the heart!* He lays bare how unspiritual they truly were. And so by missing the point, they *neglected* justice and the love of God... (- sins of omission). He even charged them for not having the love of God in their hearts, of not trusting God – consequently they did not experience the living Word, nor recognise Him when He came (Jn.5:37-42, Lk.11:39-44). By comparing them to graves, he charged them with being dead in the soul (heartless!), though apparently alive – the religious build a great facade of apparent spiritually while neglecting, and at times even oppressing those who are genuinely in need. They hide away the keys to knowing God (even by religious distractions not carrying the life of the Spirit), refusing to enter the kingdom, and stopping those who wish to! (Lk.11:52, Mt.23:13, presumably because of pride.) If we live transparently with open hearts, keeping justice and love, taking action to live out what we say we believe, there will not dwell in us the slightest notion of empty religion.

The debate on grace versus law is over when love stands up

Followers of Jesus have often focused their attention on sins of commission, (meaning things that we actively do that are wrong), when simultaneously neglecting to consider sins of omission (the things we have neglected to do). When we perceive God's heart, we realise that the sins of omission far outweigh our sins of commission! Anything stopping short of love is stopping short of Christ! The libertarians claim that they are free of the law, free to do anything and that God loves them unconditionally. Perhaps true (1 Cor.6:12), nonetheless, no Christian would happily declare themselves free of all obligation, and put their feet up while all the world around is in desperate need! The love of Christ is not satisfied simply to be free of a law which could not save us, but longs for the love that brings all to life – the Spirit makes alive! (2 Cor.3:6) This is the new and living way. We have died to the law in order to be married to the Spirit of love! (Gal.2:19) When love is in our hearts, we will not be concerned as to whether we are fulfilling a list of religious demands on us, but only – *is love being manifest all around us to the glory of God?!*

Sin exists in the absence of love, but where love abounds where can sin be found?! A hard heart is the biggest of obstructions to the presence of God (Ex.33:3); in order to harden our hearts we have to choose to reject love and in turn reject others. The Word of God clearly says that we have been made free in Christ, but He never says that He has made us free so that we can simply do what we want, what kind of a gospel is that?! What did He save us for? *We have been made free so that we are free to choose love!* Free to love from the overflow of our hearts. We have been made bondservants for Christ (1 Cor.7:22) – *love slaves!*

- We have been made free so that we can freely love -

We can also consider what the foundations of our faith look like in the light of love. This gives us a new lens to apply to every walk of life – to see it through fresh eyes. Repentance is not just having a change of heart and a change of ways, but a *turning to love* – and in this sense, did we repent far enough? – To find the place where the love of God abides? Our fire for revival will only be sustained through deeply rooted love. Our perspectives on eternity, sin and what really counts are awakened by the commission to fill the earth with the love of the Father. Our foundation of faith is greatly strengthened when rooted firmly in His everlasting love – a heart that is loved finds it easy to trust. Even the judgement is now based on what we love – *whether we love the truth or not* – this is the question (Jn.3:17-21) – will we choose the truth, or do we love ourselves or our selfish ways too much? We cannot get away from the universal thread of love that ties it all together: it is the foundation, unification and fulfilment of all His teachings.

Stunned to silence by the weight of His holiness

This presence of the Spirit of the everlasting

The life spring our well of hope

Cannot leave us defeated in our minds

When all around is the testimony His victory

Gracing us with another chance to sing: to live in His melody

Why don't these waters spill out everywhere

And all the people come to life...?

"Now am I trying to win the favour of men or God? Do I seek to please men?

If I were still seeking popularity with men, I should not be a bondservant of Christ."

Gal.1:10

Bondservants

God is seeking to bring a fresh *holiness movement* throughout the nations. The high call of God to consecration applies to all who have given themselves to following Jesus, *you are not your own* (1 Cor.6:19). We have entered into a covenant with God, in which He has given us unimaginable blessings and eternal life, yet from us He asks our all in return: we are the bondservants of Christ! I first began to see this when God called me at the age of seventeen to fully surrender my life to Him. The penny had finally dropped. One day, completely out of the blue, He spoke to me with such great power and conviction – *"Give me your whole life..."* suddenly I understood, to follow Jesus is to lay every decision at His feet, to be fully His. In this season, I began reading through the New Testament properly for the first time. So much of the New Testament carries the message of consecration, yet I had rarely heard it preached. It struck me how often the writers of the epistles referred to themselves as *bondservants*, which prompts the question – what does it mean and should we also seek to become the bondservants of the Lord?

"...if the servant says to you, I will not go away from you, because he loves you and your household, since he does well with you, then take an awl and pierce his ear through the door, and he shall be your servant always..."

Deut.15:16-17

The servant's master is so good and prospers, to the effect that the servant is compelled by love to serve Him forever. The call of God to become bondservants is genuinely for all who wish to follow Jesus. It is a call to absolute consecration, but can only be authentically fulfilled through deep love. We can have the same experience in relation to His benevolence – knowing personally the truth of His constant goodness we will choose to serve Him forever – and in this place we see the love of a bondservant. God is not calling anyone to be a bondservant without first showing them His love and His goodness (which does not negate the call!) From this place the servant loves, willing to choose surrender, and secure in love so can serve *The LORD* whole heartedly without fear. Our initial commitment to Jesus and the consecration of one's life have often been viewed as two different stages in our walk with God. The New Testament writers, and certainly Jesus made no such distinctions. Jesus taught such a strong line in regard to consecration and discipleship, calling us to it from the very beginning and clearly His call was intended for all of us.

Carrying our cross is a daily challenge

To Jesus, carrying our cross is fundamental and a daily challenge (Lk.9:23). Suffering, persecutions and the denial of the flesh are part of the lifestyle of Jesus followers (Gal.5:24). This cross is our forsaking all, being free from worthless pursuits and the desire of vain things; finding such a rich love of God, and embracing the challenge He may bring to obey Him despite our family and their expectations (Jn.14:33, 26, 27). It is not that we do not love them dearly, but that *we must obey God* and all will be tested in this way. Ultimately *love will cost us all*, hence this discipleship call. He was able to pay the ultimate price because of the joy set before Him (Heb.12:2), and surely the same will be true for us. Is discipleship a calling of high cost or deep love? The focus is not on the cost or sufferings, *but on the love gift that we are giving*. The flesh is to be crucified that we might become more sensitive to the Spirit, not forgetting that the two are diametrically opposed to one another (Gal.5:17). It is important that we recognise the purpose in all this – the grace released in the midst of our sufferings, and our need for His strength and heart for it all. The cross of our faith is an opportunity to prove our love in the midst of whatever comes, and in trials, that which is truly in our hearts is revealed (Deut.8:2). Such faith in the midst of suffering is more valuable than gold to our heavenly father (1 Pet.1:7). As we come to know through our own experience what Jesus suffered, our gratitude expands. He was made perfect through suffering (Heb.2:10) and similarly we see His greatest gift of love was given through suffering, how else will our love reach the same heights? The truth is: we are mature to the degree that we obey the Holy Spirit, the command of God, and love.

> *The focus is not on the cost or the sufferings,*
>
> *but on the love gift we are giving*

God designed this world so that one of the most precious actions in life is to stand in love continually toward someone – not just in momentary gifts or blessings, but genuinely journeying with people all the way, loving them through everything. This is why it is a call to *lay our lives down*. Family is one of the best preparations for this lifelong love walk, as we learn to keep offering this grace gift in the midst of years of commitment; this preparation is essential because *we need to treat others as family to truly love them long term*.

Jesus says – *what credit is it to you if you only love friends and family?* We have no reason to believe this is to take away from our love for family and friends – we are to love them as He does, to lay our lives down, but how far do we need to go? Was He not simply saying – *there is a greater love than the love of family and that the love of God will always reach out to others beyond these family relations.* Jesus broke the culture and expectations of His family when he stayed in the temple *to do His Father's business* (Lk.2:42-49). I believe one of the reasons Jesus taught such a hardcore discipleship line is that He wanted us to become such a people of prayer, fully accessing the depths of God and the extreme determination of the love of God. He knew the lifestyle of prayer that would be most fruitful, and that it often would cost us putting Him above the needs of our friends and family...

We have a picture before us that clearly shows that following Jesus is very costly. We also know: *the price is barely worth talking about if you're in love*. The gift of His presence far outweighs any personal cost to us that we do not even see it as cost anymore. Whilst this is true of personal sacrifices, I cannot say it extends to relational losses - the very real price we face in losing relationships or key friends, and of course the loss of our brethren to martyrdom - our love for them never dies. The distinction exists because in Christ we lose our desire for self preservation and simultaneously gain greater love for others! We feel their pain, but count our own as glory!

The cost of following Him is barely worth talking about, if you're in love...

Prophetic Perspectives

From time to time we are graced with glimpses of the future, visions of possibilities, and the intentions of God's heart. Our visions come to us piece by piece, so many questions left hanging...

What could happen if a community of lovers came forth? We could dream about this all day! A people so set on love, determined that this is all they will do – and imagine the responses from people who experience this culture of love and are drawn in. Imagine this sign of Jesus displayed clearly far and wide. Imagine a great multitude of fathers, laying their lives down for their beloved generation. Imagine an anointing for love that touches lives as we walk by – like the healing anointing Peter carried. The Holy Spirit confirms the words of His messengers with supernatural signs (Heb.2:4); what will come forth as a sign when heavenly love is abundantly displayed through us in word and deed? *Or* when we simply love on Him and watch the outpouring of the Holy Spirit all around us. It will be the true manifestation of *love wins* (Ha!) the very revelation of *the temple of love* that we are becoming. A people will arise, more impassioned for love and unity than doctrine. In stark contrast to the divisions of previous generations, these people of God – *the peace makers* will facilitate the uniting of the tribes.

As we experience more of the heart of God, we grow to love all the passions of Christ; we take on His desire to impact the world in *all* the various ways possible. We see Him everywhere we go, we learn to appreciate all the different ways He works through different people; we see Him looking to be involved in everything we do. The guidance of the Holy Spirit becomes crucial in our decision making process – to choose which visions to pursue. How can we contain His desire to fully express His heart in all the earth? Who do we choose to love first? How much resource do we deploy and how can we be most effective?

God is raising an army of peace makers

In early 2008 I was conversing with the Lord regarding how we can transition from a place of seeing momentary outpourings of the Spirit to a continual river freely flowing *(as in the days of revival)*. The fiery saints of the British Isles had set themselves to call on God over many years for the fulfilment of the many promises God has graced our nations with, not least a true revival. We had witnessed some astonishing things up until this time, yet were still so aware and hungry for the greater things the Lord was speaking of. I asked Him for a single key – *God if there is one thing that we can do to see this radical shift – into a continual outpouring, what is it?* He responded swiftly and clearly: He is planning to *reignite the prayer movement*; deep prayer will cease to be the domain of those who feel a special sense of calling to it, but the vocation of all His followers; houses of prayer will be established all over the land and they will be places of outpouring, of salvation, and of the personal discipleship of the Holy Spirit. God will train folks in the deep things of the spirit, where traditional routes have failed. Communities will spring up all around these hubs, as they become places of fellowship and deep connection with God and one another.

In times gone by there have been the most incredible graces released on groups of saints as they prayed without ceasing for hundreds of years. We can see the days now dawning, where not one holy site, but a whole multitude are springing up in unceasing prayer and worship; some of which may continue until the Lord's return. We are experiencing a transition, where the priorities of God's people are changing and the church is beginning to gather around the presence of God. No man will be able to stop this and no amount of discouragement will be able to break the hold of hope He is placing in the heart of His beloved. Whatever it was that brought these prayer movements to an end before, it will not avail again. As this hunger continues to grow, spontaneous meetings will burst forth, the worshippers will not be able to hold themselves back – we will see waves of divine invasion. These hungry souls will not be contained by their churches and will often meet in the streets. There will be such great releases of power that people will literally see Christ in us and they will conclude God is with us.

God is reigniting the prayer movement:

His people will gather around the His presence

Over ten years ago I had a profound experience through which God began redirecting my life. I was at a Christian festival one summer, and I was meditating under a tree on the last day. There was a message being given from the main tent to prepare the youth for leaving the beautiful little *bubble in a field* to enter back into normal life. In this preach an analogy was given, whereby the festival was described as the mountain (i.e. the mountain of God, as in the analogy of Moses) and we were being sent back into the valleys (normal life...) It could be very difficult in the valleys, but there was every encouragement to be ready and to trust in God. Up until this time, the youthful ups and downs of following God were the norm: incredible experiences at meetings, whilst drifting far when absent the wider community and fire filled leaders who stirred us up every summer. I wanted this year to be different. The Holy Spirit whispered to me – *what if you could live on the mountain?* What a teaser! My heart was determined that I would attempt this – to spend the kind of time with God that one does at a festival during normal life, and to pursue Him as if I was intending to live in His presence. This little whisper changed the course of my life. Believe me, I am not in the least bit criticising the message, in many ways I feel it is extremely apt – fit for purpose; and to some, the idea of living on the mountain may be a bit daunting. God knew I was ready for it and dropped me the only little temptation I needed! What does this have to do with love and prophetic futures? As we approached 2012, God placed a vision in my heart to spend a year living in His presence. To date we're in the closing months and there have been some incredible times, but I've certainly failed to prioritise it in the way He intended. One thing I have become aware of in this process is a new challenge: just like this *living on the mountain – to live in love...*

"For this reason seeing the greatness of this plan by which you are built together in Christ, I bow my knees before the Father of our Lord Jesus Christ..."

Eph.3:14

The Perfect Plan

I have often pondered upon the grand scheme of life, the big questions: an inquisitive soul seeking to understand the wisdom of God, even the answers to the *why* questions... Having sought the Lord, deliberated with friends, studied the scriptures; there was still many a question I had unresolved. As the Lord began to open His message of love to me, a fresh clarity enveloped the big picture, the puzzle was being assembled, the purposes deciphered. I recall one particular night meditating in the deep presence of the Lord, whereupon I had one of the most profound revelations I have ever experienced. The ingenuity of His plan was opened wide before my eyes. The following discourse is an exposition of the perceptions that dawned in my spirit that night.

What a glorious world love created! Love would always have done this, He couldn't resist! He chose us and would always have chosen us: this is how much He really loves us! This world is the physical and spiritual manifestation of a heart of love: He dreamed of a family and then could not resist making us. There is only this plan, this one universe: this is the expression of love, perfectly designed from the beginning. The union of the Trinity was at the heart of every aspect of their plan. They created a strategy which included a key role for each person of the Godhead; a role that they were to fulfil by being who they are, and each aspect was essential in our restoration to oneness with God. Each person of the Godhead reveals part of His heart and His nature in this plan. It was always His intention to make us one with Him and for us to be fully like Him (Rom.8:29), but in order for us to ever love, *we had to be given the choice* (consider Jesus' choice - Jn.10:17-18).

The gift of choice to us is one of the most fundamental aspects which has determined the nature of this world and God's plan for us within it. If we fail to comprehend the role of choice and its necessity, we will entirely misunderstand God.

Love is the foundation of our purpose

Having chosen the worst possible option and run as far from Him as we could, (even going to the lowest and darkest places); He showed the perfect fullness of love in bringing us back – love would not allow us to be separated from Him without an opportunity for restoration! He continued to extend His love to us, even when we had run as far as we could and rejected both His ways and His heart so completely. Once He had reconciled us to Himself (*as if that was not enough already?!*) He continued to offer us every mercy and fresh start that we could ever need. Having paid the full price for us to be reconciled to Him, He was not satisfied only that we would be clean and free of sin, but He chose to come and live in us: to walk out the journey with us. Could one be more loving? Can we question His desire to be intimate with us when He set up camp *in us?!* Could one be more loving than to come and live amongst the greatest wretches and commit to live with them until His perfection and love transform us completely?! Was it always His intention to make this a romance and a love story? Is He not so incredibly good to us that it is hard to fall out of love with Him?! Eternity is before us and we are being invited into the dance of lovers, the song of creation: to become fully wrapped up in Him – and of course this is the focus of eternity, the adventure of romance is so rich – this makes so much sense! He orchestrated this world and this plan so that we would fall *completely* in love with Him and never leave this place. When people greatly disappoint us, it seems natural that we can fall out of love, but how can one cease to love *The Faithful One?* Having experienced such depths of compassion, it becomes hard for us to imagine this journey without Him by our side.

Perhaps such a romance is not our common experience? I have to confess He has drawn me into it over time, in truth a real gift. Can we learn to be in love with God? Learn to cultivate love, to always let it grow in us and never die? When our hearts are clear of the stumbling blocks of selfishness, will not love naturally grow in the presence of the Lord...?

- He offers us every mercy and fresh start we could ever need -

It is not just the resolution of His plan in our full oneness with God that shows Love's absolute ingenuity and wisdom. He also loves us united as a people – this models the relationship of the Godhead. The glory of man united with each other through the grace of God may prove to be as great as the glory of man united with God. We will also find destiny as our hearts fall into line with His. He created a world in which all have the potential to follow what is on their heart. The heart of God in each one of us is uniquely expressed. He created us all to have a special place and contribution, and to take joy in the things of calling. The life of motivation will be released from the place of joy; we will succeed by simply being who we are (1 Jn.3:9-10 makes a connection between who we are and what we do), *just as He is does! Just as His plan from the beginning was an expression of His heart, our lives are to become an expression of our hearts. When submitted and transformed through union with God, our desires come alive in perfect destiny.* Of course this is a journey, and for the sake of our character we have a genuine battle before us.

The Holy Spirit has been encouraging me to *live from the heart* for a very long time. Scripture validates the notion that *if we are living it from the heart we are walking in the true way* (Heb.8:10, Rom.2:14-15). I have often been reluctant to embrace overly idealistic approaches to living, (which this certainly looks like,) but His persistence has been sustained over several years. God has proven to us that we are able to initiate *acts of the kingdom* purely from a place of faith and love. This was always His intention for us. As a consequence, we have seen many people healed by simply choosing to pray and believe (rather than wait on God's direction). Even the scriptures confirm to us this principle – *"the desire of the righteous brings only good."* (Pr.11:23), and *"the desire of the righteous shall be granted"* (Pr.10:24). Wisdom is given to us, to keep our hearts on track, for *"desire without knowledge is not good."* (Pr.19:2).

If we are to live from the heart, and have a heart for all men

This is some serious heart transformation!

This dynamic – of attempting to follow our heart, while waiting for His provision for the fulfilment of dreams – is an intriguing paradox. There are times when following our heart can be key in leading us to the place where we should be. Faith speaks possibilities into existence (Rom.4:17, Job.22:28). We have come to recognise character as one of the primary battles and one of the main reasons a regular surrender of our plans and dreams is so appropriate. We have a life of opportunities to love Him in the midst of life seeming incomplete, journeying through events *going wrong;* love is standing in the real world, just like when we love broken people. By continuing to trust Him through the midst of circumstances, we show Him that we do not love Him only for what He does for us.

In order to create a platform for His full glorifying in every respect – above all and beyond man – God intends to do far above our dreams and in doing so showing Himself God in this way as well (Eph.3:20). He is destined to receive the greatest glory in every sphere of life, and such He deserves!

The greatest glory is His destiny.

His destiny will be fulfilled through us

He will display His supreme wisdom in every sphere of human life

So what of this power of choice that God has delegated to us? Was giving us *choice* the greatest risk of all and the cause of the greatest destructions on the earth?

In creating a family it was always His intention that we would be fully part of the outpouring of His heart. He has planned for the bride of Christ to *fully represent Him and to fully know Him*. He could not invite us into this level of oneness without entrusting us with the potential to walk in the same level of responsibility and power as Christ. If we were not co-labouring with Him on the earth, we would not contribute in the way that He did and so not fulfil His plan (and promise) that we would be fully like Him on the earth. Also, without true choice, we could not offer real love or make sacrifices – *the cost has to be real* – else we would have nothing to offer Him at all, nothing to fight for… more than this He wanted to grant us the ultimate opportunity to offer back to Him the very lives He has given us, so He chose for us to have this ultimate responsibility, especially in regard of *the lost souls. He absolutely does not want to save the world without us* – else He would not have included us! What is the cost of this? The suffering that man has released on the world: too great for comprehension, overwhelming and heart breaking. Yet His purpose in creating a family and drawing us into this absolute oneness could not be fulfilled without the ultimate risk of *choice*. Let us be unambiguous about the implications: God did not create evil, He created choice, He gave us the power to decide, and why? – *Because He made us in His image*. Choice is integral to our nature, we would not be who we are without it. And so He intended us to be real, free people, ultimately. Perhaps I am wrong about all this, but I genuinely cannot imagine another way this could all happen… So in choosing Christ we are playing our part! And seeing this, the responsibility seems *even more compelling!* Not forgetting of course that we are responsible for *all* that we have been given and all that we know. Our common experience is to put into practice only a little of what we know we ought to do, and our excuses lack credibility, God help us!

ultimate opportunity : risk : responsibility

Why did God design our *being selfless* to be *the order of the day* and the prioritising of others? This is the one thing that guarantees our knitting together and oneness of heart! God show us our dependence on one another! He planned for the creation of family by wiring the threads of love throughout the foundations of life.

I am sure some of my friends will kick me for saying this, because it sounds too much like the responsibility lies with us, nonetheless: If we become just a little bit more radical and a little more crazy, dare to keep believing and to keep on taking risks – then everything we ever dreamed of in God can happen – isn't this what He is saying? More importantly: Everything *He has ever dreamed of* can happen, and *it is not even far beyond us… this is what His Word leads us to believe.*

- Jesus -

The Power of a Life Sold Out on Love

Imagine Jesus. Imagine a man sold out on loving and nothing else: The way that He walked supremely in love was by following the every inkling of heavens' love revealed to His heart. Imagine a devil trying to tempt this man away. The devil would find no hold -nothing, no temptation could have the smallest pull on that man's heart (Jn.14:30). This man truly believes that people are the most important thing to our heavenly Father. That by first loving Him and then them, all His plans and dreams for this world will be fulfilled in us. *A man possessed by love will stop at nothing* and we too, when the love of Christ controls and compels us, will not be deterred from seeing love manifest in all creation. When trials come, and plans fail, the purpose of the Lord will stand. When all else would give up, love keeps going, keeps hoping and keeps believing. Love will hold on to the very end: this is one of the reasons why love is the most powerful force on the face of the earth.

Imagine a man sold out on love and nothing else.

Love will stop at nothing

How does love endure all things?

Jesus gives the ultimate challenge to love. To His honour, He gave the greatest call to love mankind has ever known – His love is supreme – way beyond all other religious traditions and teachers. He calls us to love in the same way that He loved: laying down our lives *fully* for one another (Jn.13:34); this is His new command and His highest command to us – not just to give what is needed, but to give our all.

He gives us a sign of the fullness of love: *as He is, so are we in this world* (1 Jn.4:17). When we have His heart, we will see everything as an opportunity for love and for God. Jesus said categorically – if we love Him we will obey Him (Jn.14:15). Is it that acting in obedience proves our love, or is it that love will always choose obedience? Or even that love is obedience? Maybe it is all these? One thing I know is true, if we are moved by love; our obedience looks very different to that which is done only in duty. When compassion so takes over our hearts, our satisfaction is set on bringing life to people; other work can appear pointless in comparison. Love is so determined to help people, has become so altruistic, that nothing else will do.

If we walk in love we will be fully obedient

The Culture of Jesus

What is the culture of Jesus like? He does not give us a direct blueprint for culture, yet we can draw a set of key principles from His teachings. Perhaps we need to consider what *culture* is before we dive in. By *culture* we mean so many different things – traditions, arts, language, beliefs, social norms; it is a concept that we use to describe almost all of the interactions of a company of people and their collective journey together. Perhaps we should consider culture in terms of priorities, protocols and traditions? Culture is certainly not a concept centred on an individual, but we know individuals can be trend setters, culture generators, and for sure Jesus is one of these. Perhaps the most curious characteristic of His culture is the fresh and creative aspect: articulating original perspectives and truths whilst releasing miracles in a variety of new ways. A great deal of what Jesus taught was in direct contrast to both present systems and our natural inclinations, and He was clearly presenting a superior way. If love is the essence of a transcendent culture and is communicated in a way that is so powerful it re-writes the rules, it could be difficult to pin down. He sees beyond the forms and the shapes, He sees the strengths and weaknesses in them all: the essence of being *all things to all men* – becoming adaptable, versatile, *embracers of change*, lovers of diversity and is perhaps best expressed in our becoming servant of all? When Paul talks of walking out the reality of being a *servant of all* he talks in exactly the same way of becoming *all things to all men* (1 Cor.9:19-22), i.e. these are one and the same; we may even take his inference that this is *the law of Christ!*

There is a place in maturity that sees the strengths and weaknesses in every value system, every set of ideals and perspectives; it shatters all the dichotomies of left and right and the unbalanced views of idealism, recognizing that so often we need wisdom and pragmatism. In maturity, pragmatism finds a compromise between the various value sets, enabling us to break the stalemate, incorporate the whole and forge a working paradigm that transcends our individual preferences. So for example, we settle not upon an absolute socialism or individualism etc., but like so many things – our personalities, our cultures, our gifts – the corporate is best served when we meet in the middle and form something complementary. Human nature is the same the world over and as such, people have essentially the same ambitions and needs. We ought not be surprised then that God demonstrates an incredible ability to create a superior holistic culture. I wonder if the divine essence – the key element – is found in the *inclusive* and *participatory* nature of such a culture, recognizing the need for the whole and that *the full glory of God that will only come as all bring their contribution.*

So.... *the culture of Jesus?* is it definable?

If we take the sermon on the kingdom as our main reference point; Jesus focuses on our relationships with each other, our attitudes toward God and the state of our hearts. There is great benefit in looking at the relational culture He was seeking to establish; the principles He taught literally turn upside down our natural approach to relationships. He speaks of a people who give freely in every way, hold onto nothing too tightly, love all without exception, go beyond that which is expected or asked of them, have pure hearts set on all things heavenly, seek his kingdom first and by this live in peace. *How we treat people* reaches deeper than all traditions, this is the central cultural question. So if we take the same attitude as Jesus – *take cultural norms and apply the rule of the kingdom*, we will be able to communicate love whatever the customs and traditions are that surround us. We also determine that cultural norms are justly and rightly challenged when love is compromised. We see in the example – *if you are compelled to go one mile, go with him two...* Jesus is expressing how a kingdom heart is extravagant, with bold actions that communicate God's heart – *always going beyond the minimum and necessary into the generous and loving.* We see also how He did this very thing for us in the Great Covenant: He did not just forgive our sins and bring us back to Himself; He made us to have His nature and He poured out overwhelming grace and love all over us.

All the walls are coming down

In the ultimate act of *gracious subversion*, He taught us to love our enemies. How long can anyone be our enemy if we truly love them? He teaches us to exhibit *universal love;* there is no exclusion clause, no time when love is not the appropriate response, and no one who is beyond the reach of love. (Of course prophetic love often looks drastically different from our own imaginations.) Jesus made our priorities clear to us: not just to love those whom we have established relationships with or those who love us in return, but - *if you only love those who love you what reward do you have?* – it truly is for all. We can therefore legitimately call His culture a *love culture*. And it is this that is one of the distinguishing marks of Jesus followers. If we love those who love us, love those that we do not know and love our enemies; *who is left out?!*

> *"For if you love those who love you, what reward do you have?*
>
> *Do not even tax collectors do the same?"*
>
> **Mt.5:46**

Jesus spoke of the culture of the Holy Spirit, which in many ways perplexes the rational mind. For example, what do we do with the one who *does not know where he came from or where he is going?* (Jn.3:8) Are these wild moments we are called to not the reason Jesus called us to put Him first above family? How difficult is it to work with such people? Yet, *everyone who is born of the Spirit* is like this?! How do the wild spirits fit with social and family norms? We acknowledge - He did not say that we *never* know where we are going... *so how can these things coexist?* We struggle to resolve the differences. Surely the central point is simply the heart and spirit behind what we do. Maybe this is enough? Maybe there is enough power in love that cultural boundaries can freely be broken and a people united?

Folks in the Christian community have tried so hard in recent years to be cultural sensitive, and to create an environment which caters to peoples cultural preferences, to introduce Jesus to people in this context. I certainly understand the importance of connecting with people on their level, this is so important for establishing relationship – then they feel a sense of *togetherness,* developing a sense of '*we.'* And by placing the Holy Spirit in each one of us He has released the greatest resource of people to personally connect with and love all of His children in the earth. Nonetheless, the fact remains that the kingdom of God is a cultural challenge – and this kingdom expands by the expression of its own value system – love will build the kingdom, and build it far more effectively than a uniting of cultures. It is narrow minded, even short sighted for us to attempt to recreate a niche culture and try to fit Jesus in this box. A people will appear clothed in light, swimming in love, who willingly navigate all the twists and turns of culture – this is our destiny! We know that the culture of Jesus is attractive, people are drawn to the brotherhood; the testimonies shout so loud when a crew of Jesus lovers collide in a public place with folks new to this love culture.

A centre piece of this culture is the established equality of value present in every person, It is imperative that everyone is valued from the least to the greatest. This is in total contrast to celebrity culture, a separation of leaders and believers, hierarchy and the elitism that stands against the love and equality in the heart of God. *How can the culture of Jesus be exclusive when He wants us to treat the least of these as His very presence?* And let us not forget, God uses the weak and the foolish, the irrational and the unexpected to show Himself stronger and to silence the every boast of man (1 Cor.1:28-29), our faith will be entirely in God's power, not man or man's wisdom (1 Cor.2:5).

It is imperative that everyone is valued from the least to the greatest.

The people before us are a field of jewels.

No one is beyond the reach of love.

We can freely invest in everyone we meet, He loves each one supremely. Any one of us could become the greatest expression of Jesus and achieve more than all others that have walked before. Why not you? Does it depend upon the natural talents invested in us? The spiritual power of love is so great: *this alone will turn the world upside down* and all are able to love.

The Way of Jesus: Culture of the Kingdom

So in summary, He has given us a set of principles in how we are to act towards others. We know them well, God help us live it!

Treating others as we wish to be treated (Mt.7:12), Persistence (Mt.7:7), Not judging others and deciding fairly (Mt.7:1, Jn.7:24, Rom.14:13), Not worrying about practical provisions nor tomorrow – living a day at a time (Mt.6:25), Not storing up personal possessions (Mt.6:19), Serving discreetly (Mt.6:1-3), To not hide our light (Mt.5:15) – (to show forth clearly our light and the truth we know), To never stay angry but resolve matters of broken relationship as soon as possible (Mt.5:22-25), To not act towards others in lust (Mt.5:28), To bless and not curse (Rom.12:14), Not to make oaths (Mt.5:24-26), to go the extra mile (Mt.5:41) – i.e. beyond our duties or what is asked of us, never to seek revenge, or to defend ourselves (v17, 19), to be peace makers (v18), to be in readiness to forgive anything (2 Cor.2:10, Mt.18:22 - *490 times if need be!*), valuing others more highly than ourselves, even abandoning privileges we have a right to, choosing the lower place in order to raise others up (Rom.12:3, Phil.2:3-7, Col.1:24), Listening first, being slow to speak and not easily offended, i.e. one who waits, thinking before speaking, an *active* listener (Jam.1:19), putting others first – including the lowly, needy, societies outcasts and even our enemies (Rom.12:24), becoming of no reputation – becoming a servant to all, meeting the needs of the poor, giving honour where it is due (Rom.13:7), offering friendship in the Spirit of Christ, when correcting – in gentleness and not too harshly (2 Cor.2:8), not speaking evil of others (Jam.4:11), to overcome evil with good (Rom.12:21): by overflowing goodness, evil will not be able to remain...

Love: putting others first

Jesus the Worshipper

Jesus fulfilled the every command of God. He was the fulfilment of *"Love the Lord your God with all your heart ..."* What did this look like in His life? What did this look like expressed in a moment? The intensity of loving God with His whole being? What does it look like for us in worship? Have we met, seen, experienced and encountered JESUS THE WORSHIPPER, JESUS THE LOVER – overflowing with the baptism of love?!

There is no law against loving God: no law against us becoming a continual fountain of free flowing worship, (singing our hearts full out to God, and then singing His too!) We cannot love Him too much or become too radical. The only issue is to be sensitive not to neglect the love of others. However, to seek Him to the point of neglecting to love others is certainly difficult, hard to miss when Holy Spirit is so keen on us doing this – i.e. *we need not worry about being too radical in prayer and worship.*

With regard to worship and the presence of the Lord, I sensed such a challenge in writing this: considering all worshippers (leaders or otherwise,) who know *the song of worship*: we know the way – He is enthroned on the praises of His people, we all know how to find Him and how to worship Him; we know He can't resist a song of praise from a pure and sincere heart. *No matter what it sounds like to man, He cannot resist it, we all know this!* Yet somehow – how have we not done more to prioritise His presence – do we really know this? Have we heard the call of God to live in His presence? Do we see this as the fulfilling of His heart's desires? *(I digress...)*

Jesus describes how the Father expresses His love to the Son and in doing so He shows Him *everything* that He is doing (Jn.5:20). Jesus called us friends, sharing all that God was sharing with Him – *"I have called you My friends* because I have made known to you everything that I have heard from My Father" (Jn.15:15). No doubt as we draw near we will begin to see more and more of the things on His heart that He is seeking to do all around us, for our locality. *What if, as His friends we always knew what He was doing?!*

At the same time, Jesus talks in a way that indicates He couldn't function without the Father, Holy Spirit and prophetic vision (Jn.5:19, 30). In one sense we could say He was *ruined* like many of us have become – *God's will must be done, I must know Him, nothing matters more.* When our hearts become set on Him it can look like this. Furthermore, *"My food is to do the will of Him who sent me"* (Jn.4:34); His will is to bring life to others: we find sustenance in bringing life to others.

When we consider Jesus life, we often focus on the death and resurrection as His ultimate gift to us, without which we would not be saved. Using this reference frame however, it would be easy to underestimate the cost and love given in living thirty three years on this earth in pure obedience to the Father. No doubt the cross was overwhelmingly difficult and the most intense suffering anyone has ever been through; my point is simply that love was sown throughout His life without end.

Jesus: thirty three years on the earth in pure obedience to the Father

This is worship.

Greater Love Has No Man than This

In the life and death of Jesus Christ, God set a new bar for love; He redefined what love looks like in an unprecedented way. Never before had the heart of God been revealed so profoundly and completely – this was the time in all eternity where God revealed His heart fully and played His ultimate hand. In the eyes of God, He has proved His supreme love through dying for us – while we were still sinners (Rom.5:8-10, Eph.2:4-7). Would we be willing to die for another who does not know Him, even one who is caught up in a life of wickedness? God regards that no man has greater life than to give his life for another and He calls us to lay our lives down in the same way that He did (Jn.15:12-13). Interestingly, at this point He says *"You are my friends if you keep on doing the things which I command you to do"* (14).

Maybe the greatest grace is to always live in love

– One Big Happy Family –

A Generation of Fathers

In 2011 the Lord started to impart His vision to me to raise a generation of spiritual fathers. It would be fair to say that true spiritual fathers in the previous generations are few, rare and great treasures. As this spiritual awakening continues to progress, more fathers continue to appear. I was seeking the Lord for a time that He might raise up true fathers all across the land; the question He laid before me was quite simple, *what if we were to raise an entire generation of fathers?* If being a spiritual father became the norm in our generation it would have one of the most profound impacts on the following generation growing up, not to mention the whole of society. For many people parenting is their most significant leading role in life, yet we rarely match this in terms of training or validation. As callings go, training a generation of spiritual fathers seems to be one of the most important things that the Lord has ever laid before us. I consider it so crucial that we ought to consider it one of our highest priorities – and devote both time and heart to understanding what it means to be a true father, so that we can fulfil this calling as best we can...

A great deal of what constitutes fathering well consists in the development of good relationships. In addition there are specific roles and attributes that we anticipate should be present in the lives of father figures. In our natural understanding, they are those who protect us, create safety, guide and lead us (and for a lot of people feeling safe is a prerequisite to feeling loved). If we consider how much love, support and personal attention every child needs, it was clearly the design of Genius for mankind to have a small number of children for every set of natural parents.

When we consider, *who are our true spiritual parents?* We often look up particularly to those who have walked the roads we are called to walk. The great honour of carrying wisdom is passing it on to the next generation; one of the foremost elements of fathering is sharing life experience. We identify those who carry the wisdom, character and understanding that we value and need as fulfilling these roles, knowing also that it is the role of parents to recognise our gifts and callings and help us train for them. Spiritual parents will be most effective when they create both relationship and culture which genuinely feels like family. People are greatly encouraged when those they respect and seek to emulate encourage them and provide a reassuring presence in their lives. Knowing that you have people watching over you who genuinely know the Lord, and are there for you if ever you need them, goes a long way to putting us at rest and making us feel safe. As spiritual parents in training, we must cultivate our gifts of discernment and assist the youth in finding their way in God (their path, their calling). Many of the relational aspects of fathering well are not discussed in this section in any great detail as they are not substantially different from the general principles of creating good relationships (– which are discussed in other chapters of this book). I imagine it is obvious by now that I believe in keeping things simple, in applying what Jesus taught and in loving and obeying the Holy Spirit. If we do this, we are destined to become the most effective spiritual parents we can be. In addition, one of our highest aspirations should be to thoroughly get to know the people of God we are walking with (Pr.27:23) – to *really* know them, and then to treat them in accordance with their maturity; this subject is briefly covered in the exploration of leadership styles later on.

So what is it that distinguishes spiritual fathers from leaders or teachers?

The heart of a parent is much greater than the heart of a leader: the distinction centres on priorities. In natural relationships we see paternal and maternal instinct – the intrinsic love parents often carry, which produces the natural parental response – to put their children first. They see their role and responsibility as the success of their children: life becomes far more about their children than their own success. This is not dissimilar from Jesus' call to *put others first, period* (Phil.2:3-5). One thing that is definitely true about every spiritual father I have ever been close to is the deep sense of love that they have for people. As those who are mature in the faith, all true fathers carry a lot of love; this can be one of the most distinctive marks that distinguishes them – fathers will literally lay their lives down for their families.

As regards the focus and goals of fathers, it is not one of *follow my vision* (as we so often see), but their desire is to see the visions of others fulfilled first. They openly share all they have to aid their children going as far as they possibly can. Some even seek to do everything in their power to ensure the next generation have the best preparations possible for whatever they may pursue. Furthermore, fathers are keen that *all* of the diverse visions, hearts and ideas of the people are represented and pursued – showing no favouritism (Jam.1:17, Col.3:25).

Fathers long to create to a home for all

To become a real spiritual father, knowing *The Father* personally is imperative. By treating people in the same way that He fathers us we best fulfil this function. Of course the idea of a father figure to whom people look up to, contains all the usual connotations we would expect – being above reproach in character (Eph.1:4, 1 Tim.3:2), worthy of emulating (1 Cor.11:1) – and for sure great role models are presently in short supply! As fathers we choose to treat people as our literal family – God has taught us such (1 Tim.5:1-2), and we have an example in Paul – he considered Timothy a true son (1 Tim.1:2). When people become our family a very different relationship is established from an institutional one. In institutions people have distinct roles through which they interact and the relationship is often one way; hierarchical systems frequently dominate; the relationship may be temporary – only for a season; whereas in family we view every relationship as potentially lifelong. As a family we see our success as inter-related and that we are somewhat dependent on another. Our relationships are viewed as paramount to our roles and gifts; there is a togetherness that cannot be broken. There is also a certain humility present in *"be subject to one another out of reverence for Christ."* (Eph.5:21), God can reveal anything to any one of us and let us be humble enough to receive from the Lord through anyone. God has positioned leaders to guide the ship, rather than be the sole source of creative vision. How much greater are the fruits of listening to what God is saying through all His people? It is interesting that Paul considered himself the least of all the apostles (1 Cor.15:9), the chief of sinners (1 Tim.1:15) and did not over value his own importance (Rom.12:3, Lk.14:10-11). In fact, love will be willing to become the lowest and to become of no reputation for the sake of others (Phil.2:7) – servant of all!

God is calling us to treat people as family

Family is one of the primary areas God uses to train us for love. In the first command to *"honour your mother and father;"* (Ex.20:12) God gives us an opportunity to love without condition – to choose to love our parents regardless of how they treat us. We know that Jesus challenges us to love people regardless of their attitude toward us because of His command to *'love your enemies'* and then again through Peter in regard to loving those in authority who treat us harshly (1 Pet.2:18-21). Perhaps the point here is again – *His love will win them all over!*

Let us not forget that *all leadership is connected to responsibility*, those who take the lead carry responsibility for others. We should be careful therefore to recognise or to appoint people who take their responsibilities seriously and who put others first above themselves. Let it be as Jesus said, *"whoever wishes to be first among you must be your servant, and whoever desires to be first among you must be your slave"* (Mt.20:26-28). One has to wonder what dynamic would occur if we taught young leaders – *we are looking to appoint slaves for Christ!*

Fathers lead first by example

One of the primary roles of parents is to be an example to others, and one worthy of following. As a father Paul committed himself to never be a burden to others (2 Cor.11:9), and to lead by example, even working to support himself in line with this. It is hard to imagine him giving an offering pitch to support his 'ministry' like the ones we so often hear today... He was ready to give all he had for his children, this is no small heart!

"...I will not burden you [financially], for it is not your [money] that I want but you; for children are not duty bound to lay up store for their parents, but parents for their children. But I will most gladly spend [myself] and be utterly spent for your souls. If I love you exceedingly, am I to be loved [by you] the less"

2 Cor.12:14-15

"After all, though you should have ten thousand teachers in Christ, yet you do not have many fathers... so I urge and implore you, be imitators of me.

1 Cor.4:15-16*

When we consider the role of fathers, we have often pondered how significant they are in determining the direction of a generation. True fathers make such a deep impact on young people – being such a source of inspiration, encouragement and vision. There is such a sense of safety and respect generated when fathers have *been this way before* and are looking out for us; in this sense they are those who carry great wisdom from both spiritual depth and life experience. Prophetic voices have been indicating for years that we are on the threshold of one of the greatest moves of God of all time; this move is destined to be carried by a multitude of fathers!

There is an Elijah calling to *turn the hearts of the fathers to the children and children to the fathers*. Such was peculiarly evidenced in the life of John the Baptist, a wilderness wanderer, given for the turning and preparation of his generation. When the hearts of fathers are turned away, we are in danger of finding a generation of lost youth. Youth are very perceptive; they can see whether people's hearts are turned towards them. All true fathers place great value on children – this is one of the clear distinctions between true fathers and others who are simply leaders – this posture of the heart: whether in truth the heart is set toward the young and those for whom we have been given responsibility.

Are we carrying the youth of today in our hearts?

In the absence of fathers, God met many of us in our youth and drew us into a deep communion – promising to fulfil all the key roles – coach, mentor, father, teacher... I have no doubt He will continue to do this for many in the coming generation; nonetheless there is a strong call resounding out from the heavens – God is calling fathers, He desires to train a whole company to father the people of the earth and knowing it may take some years to learn and train, we ought embrace this call now. *Of course it equally applies to mothers in the spirit no less.* Oh God – that a multitude of mature spiritual parents would arise in our generation!

"And he will go before him in the spirit and power of Elijah to turn back the hearts of the fathers to the children, and the disobedient... to the wisdom of the just – in order to make ready for the Lord a people prepared."

Lk.1:17

Whilst we have not examined the various specifics of how fathers outwork their roles, there is one aspect that we cannot fail to consider: *discipline;* it is an essential part of the role of all fathers and we see this in God's relationship to us (Heb.12:7). Discipline is often viewed by our unrenewed minds in a negative fashion as it stands as a check to the soul. The truth is, *right discipline comes from love desiring the best for others;* this is commonly not in line with our feelings, desires, or in the timing we wish. Self-control is a fruit of the Spirit (Gal.5:23), we know that we need it! Without discipline and tribulations we would never become fully mature people (Rom.5:3-5) and as such God will never abandon it in all our days. One of the fundamental reasons He holds off from giving us what we ask for immediately is to prioritise character development. He knows what is best for us, and He loves us too much to make it too easy. Paul embraced personal discipline no end, choosing to buffet his own body, and he faced much discipline through trials! (1 Cor.9:27) Furthermore, he regarded that godliness affects everything in our lives and as such, training ourselves toward godliness through spiritual disciplines will reap no end of fruit (1 Tim.4:7-8).

Before speaking into peoples' lives, we should consider whether we have the right to, has it been invited? Is it desired? Is this the best way? If we show people honour and communicate our respect of their equal value and autonomy, our guidance will be more easily received. As fathers we ought not to shy away from being directive *if* the occasion demands; but always to be directive from a moral basis, *i.e. when it is simply the right thing for them to do.* This is true whether it is our inclination or otherwise (offering suggestions in wisdom is usually enough if a heart is soft to learn). In the context of proper respect, it is a benefit to us all to have directive people looking out for us. The Lord is extremely directive at times, and without a doubt Paul wrote clear and firm instructions to those whom he loved. The occasion when we need be directive should still nonetheless be rare. People have to make their own choices, even after we advise them, and it is best for them that they do. The misplaced desire people may carry to *follow another man,* should be challenged. Our aim is to help people stand on their own feet – to encourage growth through the exercise of their own initiative and discernment, but they need opportunities. If we have led well by example, and encouraged true wisdom, the people we influence will always look to the wise and the elder for guidance and counsel when needed. Discipline and counsel are forever guardians of life's pathways. Are we postulated ready to share all of life's lessons openly and freely? – To share anything and everything if it will benefit the rising generation?

Friendship

It is my personal belief that the calling of God to befriend people is a highly significant one. This calling ought to take precedence over our commitment to institutions. Our relationships with Institutions are often temporary or seasonal, whereas the friendships we are building with our brothers and sisters are not only for life, but will go on for eternity. God is building friendships in our lives which will stand every test and will never be broken. When we take an approach that sees anyone as a potential friend and partner in life, regardless of their allegiances, we give ourselves the best opportunities to build real friendships – a diverse, organic network. People come to know that we are genuine and that we consider them of real value when we demonstrate that they are our priority and not the growth of an institution.

Real friends can sometimes be few and far between, absolute gems when we find them and the basis for some of the richest fellowship we can ever enjoy. There have been far too many tragic stories of people moving on from churches (or other organisations) for legitimate reasons, only to find that the people they had been journeying with for years were not their true friends and made little or no effort to stay in touch when they left. Thank God – in most of the cases I have personally heard of, these people had other friends outside these spheres that stood by them and were a real help through those difficult times. People are searching for real companionship and connection, for substance and depth. Many people in the earth have never had true friends. In an era when society is considerably fragmented, and when many folks lack stability, (for a whole variety of reasons), we can be an incredible help to people by simply extending the hand of friendship. We should also aim to be sensitive to the growing population of singles, since a stable network of friends is all the more crucial for them, especially if they do not have close family relationships. We will proceed by asking the question – what does it mean to be a real friend?

- A friend loves at all times -

Prov.17:17

What a glory it is to God:

When friends stand side by side through thick and thin!

Isn't the one who loves at all times also the one that everyone wants to be friends with? Imagine people never let us down, always stuck to their word, were sensitive to other's needs before their own... *would living in community be so difficult then?*

Put people together who have well functioning friendships both relating and communicating well, and the community will thrive with little input and effort. The truth is: we find it easier to love someone to the degree that they are standing in love. In my experience, our immaturity is the main hindrance to our walking together – an apparent selfishness which stands in the way. If we follow the principles *The Book* teaches us, a natural loving community will spring up. Where a mature company gathers, a glorious harmony develops.

True there are a number of relational skills we need to master in order to make this work: communication (listening and speaking clearly), patience (giving each other grace, being flexible), the giving of love. Without a doubt there is a choice and cost to developing both friendships and communities and on some level we have to wonder if in their absence there is a lack of will: how far are we willing to go? What of the cost of time?

"Let your love be sincere."

A good friend is available and approachable, focused on the other person (even giving their whole attention), values them highly – above themselves (Phil.2:3, we have equal standing!), is committed and a ready, careful listener. A good friend will be tenderhearted, of a humble and gentle spirit, full of love, patient, ready to forgive anything (Col.3:12-13), responsive and not reactive, supportive and not contentious, the very voice of encouragement!

"And above all these put on love and enfold yourselves with the bond of perfectness."

Col.3:14

The essential depth of close relationship is found in journeying together. The exchange of dialogue through a lifetime of adventures is a real treasure. An openness of heart is offered – a transparency, where in trust we make ourselves vulnerable and share our true selves. The safety of love allows us to drop all our boundaries, and expose our broken selves in a full deep honesty. True friendship is choosing to love someone knowing fully who they are. Deep shared experiences can have the effect of building profoundly strong bonds: we have a shared journey and experience which binds us together. The level of honesty that develops in these relationships enables us to have the full blessings of each other's insights In accord with the proverbs: *"faithful are the wounds of a friend"*, and *"as iron sharpens iron: so a man sharpens the countenance of his friend"* (Pr.27:6, 9, 17).

"There is a friend that sticks closer than a brother."

Pr.18:24

When trouble comes, you know who your real friends are. If we are engaged in helping those in need, many will be won over as our friends. Deep bonds form in the midst of hardship. And how much of a blessing is the comfort of a friend in a time of need?

- A brother is born for adversity -

How far do we take the encouragement to become a *friend to sinners?* The Lord even said to me one day – *making disciples is making friends.* Does He mean that we should do our best to be the friend of all? Or simply that *we should treat people in the spirit of friendship,* even if they do not reciprocate? Can we learn to be sensitive to people so that we do not cause them to close their hearts from us unnecessarily? The gospel is offensive enough already, without our adding our own barriers! We know that the lack of manifestation of love is one of the primary reasons that more fruit has not come in the last generation. Surely if our gospel is to bring *life to all men,* and primarily seeking to love, we need not worry about our being 'religious' at all.

If we consider how love is expressed in our *sharing the truth of Jesus* with people, we carry surprisingly varying perspectives and approaches. I have no doubt that love, aware of impending troubles ahead, will not fail to give a *warning*; love will find the boldness needed to confront difficult issues, even to warn people! Does it not make every effort to seek out the best for others? What lengths will we go to find ways to communicate that are clearly understood – in a way that each person can engage with? How about painting a thousand fresh allegories in the hope that *one dream might capture the heart.* I wonder if – when love is clearly displayed in the public sphere, people will not need to be told *the gospel is about love!*

A heavenly culture dwells amongst a collective opening its arms wide to the strangers that cross our paths. Creating a welcoming, friendly culture is one of the first steps we can take to encourage people to open their hearts to us. At times we will need to sacrifice time with our beloved friends in order to embrace new folks, through which the greater good is also served. Key relationships can still be identified and prioritised. One of the big issues we face today is – what can we do when our lives are already full? After all, the proverb is sometimes translated: *"The man of many friends will prove himself a bad friend"* (Pr.18:24). We know that folks in need can take a lot of our time to serve well, and often it seems like we are loving them to no avail, particularly if they seem ungrateful. No doubt God sees how we treat them as how we treat Him, and values it all the same. I wonder if there is a way to *love people to life* and that as a result even the very goodness of God will come forth as a living stream?!

Practical generosity is one of the primary ways we can show love to people that we do not know; it is unsurprising then that we are charged to never neglect it (Heb.13:2); people can decline generosity, but cannot deny it. How much greater is the culture of generosity when it is expressed more widely than the usual practical means – generosity of heart and spirit, a true openness.

Do we see everyone as valuable regardless of their contribution?

It's not so hard, it's really not so hard to love

Fixing the Breaks

We have looked at some of the key aspects of healthy relationships: in fathering, in friendship, in the example of Jesus life. Before we proceed to consider community dynamics, we will consider the negatives – what happens when relationships are strained, why and what can we do about it? My intention is that we develop our understanding in accord with the saying *prevention is better than cure.* By learning the positives and implementing them – what is good and right, and establishing beneficial approaches, there is a greatly diminished need to deal with the negatives. If we establish a culture which fixes the smallest of disparities before they grow into substantial tensions we can prevent the majority of relational breaks. What we find is, relationships are not so difficult to do well as we sometimes imagine; and when seeing successful relationships flourishing it is a strong testament to this.

It is hard to fall out with people who are difficult to offend. Those who live *at peace* are the most difficult of all to upset and curiously, those who love the truth – *the Word of God*, cannot be offended (Ps.119:165). What character traits always coexist with a love of the truth? People who are secure in themselves are most at peace, and unlikely to wrongly perceive a personal attack when not intended. Offences often come because of a perceived attack on one's person: values or identity. A defensive position is adopted in the midst of pain and the walls are raised. Those who hurt others often do so from a state of personal brokenness. Once we find a place of wholeness and security in who we are, we no longer need an outlet for our pain or to fight for ourselves. Overreactions and disproportionate responses are most commonly caused by touching on sensitive areas and open wounds, albeit accidentally. Without contention, those who are hardest to offend are easiest to reconcile with. Wisdom will find ways to prevent offences as much as possible, for *a brother offended is harder to win than a strong city* (Pr.18:19, NKJV).

"Strip off bad feeling towards others."

Col.3:8

One of the key observations we find in this relational journey, is that people who *love first* are far more interested in restoring a relationship than accurately assigning blame or thrashing out the fine details of what went wrong. When we value our relationships more highly than our own pride, we will always seek reconciliation above the determination of fault, justifications and reputation. Those who value their friends most deeply will seek to prevent anything from ever coming between them – will check everything is ok, go the extra mile in communication and care, and seek to resolve any conflict as quickly and thoroughly as possible. We are more grieved at the break in the relationship and aware of our liability to miss the mark; we will admit our errors freely without objection, calling on grace for healing and prevention of future failures. When we are thoroughly gracious with each other, we want to admit our wrongs, we want to confess our mistakes and ask for forgiveness – ever ready to hold our hands up, ever reluctant to defend ourselves – because we want union with our friends restored first and foremost.

Breaks in relationships most commonly occur due to our misunderstanding and bad communication, so we must adopt the position –*we need to learn to communicate better*. Never pointing the finger or dividing – because this is *never helpful,* so we simply apologise. We even find that coming together in love fixes problems to the degree that a thorough sorting out is not always necessary – in the same way that His manifest love and presence causes us to feel the sense of restored union without us confessing our every mistake first.

At these times we try to hold in view God's desire for our union and the greater power it releases, and more than this acknowledging – we need each other! The position of humility is one which does not anger quickly or seek to justify itself, and its soft words turn away wrath (Pr.15:1); care is taken so as not to create a big issue out of small things of little importance. When communicating over misunderstandings, we seek to be clear as to what our perceptions and feelings are versus absolute truth or facts – having the humility to recognise our limitations.

Seeking to understand the perspectives and value systems of others is a foundation stone for all conflict resolution. Furthermore, we make every effort to reconcile, even in the midst of being treated wrongfully, willingly taking the blame unjustly at times in the hope of mended hearts...

We are on the same team

Let us never lose sight of this

Disagreements and misunderstandings are ever easier to fix when the fundamental love, trust and value in a relationship is well established – when you know someone ultimately cares about you and values you, you know that they have your best interests at heart – and therefore can be trusted: it creates an atmosphere for vulnerability, for honesty, for expressing our feelings and concerns; we can get everything out in the open and actually deal with it. We can talk about our perceptions and feelings without concern of insecurities creating misunderstandings or the value of either the relationship or individual being brought into question. This is the safety of love.

There is always a grace to love people

One of the most helpful principles I have discovered is to view any relationship with collective responsibility and ownership: it is *our* relationship. All the time that we can recognise breaks as our joint problem to resolve, we can stand together and find ways to work it out (Pr.17:14). As soon as we allow the pain of discord to divide us into *'you and I'* (or worse *'you vs me'* !?) as if on other sides of a battle, we have made the first error in allowing an incident to separate us. It is not always the provocation in the incident which is the fundamental problem, but frequently something deeper. For sure where offences lie unhealed they spring up in the midst of discord. This is partly why I favour the open hearted approach: keeping things in the light, with short accounts, clarifying at times to the nth degree if needed (we could risk communicating too well, rather than the opposite). Misconceptions are easily developed, body language misread, things taken personally which were never intended (assumptions producing unintended interpretations – when clarifications are not given – *let's stop assuming!*). If we talk openly and clearly, we can prevent all of these issues which spring up in the midst of the unsaid. We will do well to affirm the love we have for our brothers and sisters, regularly and deeply: to the point where it cannot be doubted. Established trust through love should be a primary goal in the early stages of any relationship. Learning to understand one another, interpret the meaning of what is said, communicating clearly and sharing hearts. Such will provide a stable foundation for a good and healthy relationship. *God help us!*

Resolving conflict is our shared responsibility

A simple discipline we can exercise that yields a great fruitful union with little cost, is the discipline of regularly checking on each other – Are you ok? Are we ok? By doing this we communicate our pursuit of our friend and that we have their back. This regular contact goes a long way to prevent issues developing, since the small differences can be quickly dealt with (are we really ok?), the precedent is one where the relationship is prioritised and protected, matters of concern are not left unsaid and therefore cannot build up (Pr.17:14).

Hardness of heart is the pride that pulls people apart; in one sense it is the absence of love, an emptiness that chooses loneliness. Sin is fundamentally selfish and quenches love. In the context of a sinful culture, the love of a great body may grow cold (Mt.24:12). *Staying out of sin is all about staying in love:* there is no sin in love (1 Jn.2:10). Commitment gives love in the fullest *and protects it*; whereas impurity compromises it, *blocking communication and communion*. We know that purity and maturity walk together, and *the pure in heart will see God.*

Our hearts become soft in the presence of God. When we confess our wrongs and adopt a position of humility we soften further. There are keys to keeping a soft heart: keeping short accounts, dealing with issues as they arise, approaching each other in honesty and transparency. If we are unwilling to hold onto things, and wish to fix them as soon as we can, we cannot carry baggage. When trust is broken the natural response (and temptation) is to close our hearts or walk away – to protect ourselves. It is far better, that even embracing the cross of Christ, we face the pain, fight down the inclination to build walls and close our hearts, in order to maintain an attitude of openness and love.

To say that love goes the extra mile is barely the beginning...

Love often goes as far as it can.

Perhaps I am wrong, but I believe that a person walking in maturity of character, with the power of love and the wisdom of God can always find a way to communicate, understand and aid healing in any broken relationship;

even if one party is terrible at communicating and offences exist. There is something ever so powerful about extending grace and love to someone – it is ultimately disarming, it offers value and affection – such that insecurities fade away. *You can't argue with the love of God.*

You can't argue with the love of God

If we are looking to love, we will not be looking to judge, these two are mutually exclusive. Those who walk full in love are not able to judge the wrong way – *love can never stop at an assessment of the state of things, or condemnation.* It will always look to help to assist and make better – can't help wanting to – to bring life when things fall short. When love sees something amiss: it responds, it acts – it is active not passive, *it cannot stay passive.* Love is so determined to express itself it is set on guiding, correcting and challenging us back to love. If someone makes a serious error, the loving one will not simply accept *'this is how they are,'* choosing rather to focus on their potential – *who they are becoming.* To accept *'this is just how they are,'* as if they will always be this way is to judge them. This kind of judgement arises from unbelief. The heart that judges wrongfully identifies weaknesses, mistakes, errors – and does not seek to assist, but rather points to these issues and raises them up, even unto confrontation, instead of extending grace or mercy. Confrontation can of course be positive – *I love you too much to let things stay this way,* born out of our commitment to pull down discord and deceptions. The failure to act in the midst of seeing others' weaknesses, (even if simply to come to prayer,) comes from an absence of the heart of God.

There are a few basic mistakes that have often been made when dealing with the errors of others: to negate to appreciate the circumstances of the past (– there are always reasons why people are drawn to make bad choices and most folks need healing,) to fail to look heavenwards expectant for the redemptive grace of God to be outpoured in the midst of their error; and lastly as Jesus so aptly taught us – *let he who is without sin cast the first stone* (Jn.8:7, Gal.6:1) – we should deal with it humbly and graciously, knowing we could make the very same mistakes. Love sets itself on finding the solutions, on being the answers for others, *never* to add to their struggle.

I have often pondered on why we cling so tightly to our beliefs and value systems, and sometimes relatively little to each other. Why are we so ready to contend and fight about priorities? Why do we hold our convictions so strongly about small details, many of which are irrelevant in the big scheme of things? Or even circumstances that we have little power over. Is it just pride? I realise we are compelled to live by our convictions regarding the truth, and truth is certainly important, but in God the conviction to love is equally strong and binds us together. As regards our convictions, we are encouraged to keep them between us and God if needed for the love of others (Rom.14:22).

The expectations that stem from our worldviews, personalities, perspectives and experiences of life may be wildly different from one another. Our value systems and priorities reflect these differences. We are surprised to find that this can be equally true of believers in Jesus as it is in other walks of life despite all that we have to unite over. The hopes that any particular group of people choose to invest in vary enormously. We rarely sit down and discuss our hopes and expectations, yet they can be the very thing we draw from which produces conflict. We are taking a substantial relational risk if we neglect to voice what we truly value. We can only truly know and understand someone when we appreciate what they value and dream for, and why. As a consequence of this, we should prioritise discussion of our values and expectations in all our key relationships and be careful not to make unfounded assumptions. Disappointments commonly arise from blocked goals, unmet needs and failed hopes – especially when they have not been communicated. When we are communicating our expectations of one another, we should always ask ourselves – are these expectations realistic and fair?

We see how differently we respond to this 'value system' dynamic when we strike up a good friendship without knowing a person's convictions and beliefs. Time and time again people find such a strong sense of appreciation, connection and enjoyment of another's company, only to later discover that they hold strong convictions in contradiction to ours. The challenge stands before us, that upon discovering such differences of perspective, we do not allow the relationship to be damaged or compromised. In fact, this dynamic is one of the key experiences in life that teaches us to extend tolerance and acceptance, not to judge people on appearances and to seek to cultivate friendships in unfamiliar circles. How many cultural stereotypes and errant beliefs about people groups have been destroyed through our overcoming these apparent barriers and building diverse friendships outside of our comfortable norms? - Refusing to deny the fundamental of human solidarity or to believe the separatist lies which stand at the core of sectarian divisions. Are we trying to surround ourselves with people just like ourselves? Surely love in full maturity will become indiscriminant, never judging by the sight of our eyes or cultural stereotypes? The heart can find the heavenly road, far beyond curbing our predisposed judgements, living in the land where the judgemental thought based on perceptions of categorizations - colour, creed, gender and the like, simply does not exist.

The challenge of love can be the very challenge of the cross – for all involved.

"Bear one another's burdens and troublesome moral faults, and in this way fulfil and observe perfectly the law of Christ..."

Gal.6:2*

"Living as becomes you] with complete lowliness of mind (humility) and meekness (unselfishness, gentleness, mildness), with patience, bearing with one another and making allowances because you love one another. Be eager and strive earnestly to guard and keep the harmony and oneness of [and produced by] the Spirit in the binding power of peace."

Eph.4:2-3

"Above all things have intense and unfailing love

for one another, for love covers a multitude of sins"

1 Pet.4:8

Grace is one of the most powerful agents at holding relationships together. Those with enduring love and patience can find the ability in God to serve anyone in the midst of their need. As a friend once said to me *'the kingdom of God is always messy,'* we were discussing the outworking of community and she was explaining how people can be in a real state when they enter into the kingdom of God! More than this: some are the most difficult to work with, at times resistant to change (even defiant). *To keep standing in love towards someone* can be the greatest of miracles. Thank God He's big enough to love everyone no matter how hard our hearts have become or how unwilling we are to change. We can see these hardened, broken folks through the lenses of His love: prophetically seeing them as He does in all the potential and fullness of Christ. What greater relational prophetic experience can we have than to see someone in the eyes of love? We are empowered through His vision to treat them as Christ and so bring life to them, pulling them out of whatever dark holes they have become entangled in. Our role is always to bring light, life and love. We need not always concern ourselves with why there are issues, simply come to the solution – *come to God!*

As regards communication, we typically underestimate how much information and explanation is sufficient in order to be properly understood;

or we are unaware of how much more beneficial *a little more* communication can be to the other party. This may be due to a common tendency to make inaccurate assumptions. Are we willing to take the time to fully explain ourselves as a service to others? Miscommunication has been the failure of so many relationships, which is why we should be wise to this and prioritise the discipline and development of these skills. There is a level of mutual understanding which can be reached between two parties whereupon both are fully understood by each other; this is the place we need to reach. Checking what each other intends by a use of phrase or particular words can also be extremely valuable – people commonly use language in different ways and many an argument has occurred because of a very different understanding of a few words. We have varied emotional attachments to words – historical connotations or precedent can unfortunately be profoundly different. Giving someone the benefit of the doubt is a gift of grace and can be the difference between resolution or otherwise.

The Lord has set His heart on us and will not be deterred or give up. He is our example to follow. It is particularly hard for us to do this with those who consistently hurt us and do not want to change, we feel like giving up. Nonetheless the Lord's challenge to us stands: to treat others in the way that He treats us:

> *"I will not in any way fail you nor give you up*
> *nor leave you without support..."*
>
> **Heb.13:5**

Or as Jonathan Helser beautifully put it:

> *"I'm never giving up on you."*

Imagine a community of lovers living in the oneness of God

Articles of Harmony

In the spring of 2012 I wrote an article attempting to voice God's heart and desire for oneness and harmony in our generation. This article seems a suitable introduction to this section on community, though it does repeat some of what has already been said. Nonetheless, a little repetition is sometimes helpful. I have reproduced the article below as a second edition with some parts rewritten:

"Neither for these alone do I pray, but also for all those who will ever come to believe in Me through their word and teaching, that they all may be one, as You Father are in Me and I in You, that they also may be one in Us, so that the world may believe and be convinced that You have sent me"

Jn.17:20-21

Jesus prayed that His people would be one, but not just one with each other – He was very specific – He prayed that we would be one *just as the Godhead is one*. I love to ponder on what this means, what does it look like? It exists right now and – *can we see this emerge ourselves* and so become like God in this? The Father, Son & Holy Spirit all have roles. They relate to each other and to us through these; yet they stand as three persons, distinct, yet fully perfect and in harmony. To me this is one of the most powerful aspects of God's redemption in Christ and would be one of the most glorious things to ever see and be a part of – that we would be one in the same way. Imagine that the people of God might find that perfection of harmony. And Jesus prays that this will happen – are the prayers of Jesus in vain?! Are they the will of God?!

I have become convinced that God intends to fulfil every possibility that Christ has made available somewhere on the earth. As the Bride of Christ we are to take on His heart for harmony and oneness. So here I am waving to God (and do join me!) – *Hey, I want to be a part of this one!!! Don't let me miss out here!*

What did Jesus pray? and did He pray in faith believing the Father would fulfil His prayers?

> *"that they all may be one in us, so that the world may believe..."*

If we read this correctly, it has to indicate a timing prior to the return of Christ – the world will already know the truth of God revealed in the end, so the implications of *'so that the world may believe'* would be irrelevant. If we take the view that the Lord is to return at the time when the last man is saved, the establishment of His Unity in us must be a key aspect in the salvation of the world. We also see that He was praying for *all that would come to believe*, i.e. the unity of the Trinity could potentially be manifest in every generation! God let it be in ours!

And here's the thing: how much glory is there in the unity and love of a company of people? Over a number of years God has been revealing to me His vision for family, community and harmony. I have begun to see again and again that this is one of the great glories in all of time, and I am lost for words to describe it. I cannot overstate how powerful this is. It ties into the power of love itself and its purest manifestation.

How much glory is there in the unity and love of a company of people?

So, *how will it happen?*

I've learned to try to take a pragmatic perspective to vision – after years of seeing visions of the future and of the possibilities of Christ – and in the midst of not seeing some of them fulfilled, one begins to ask – Lord, how will this happen? Is it timing? Is there anything we can do? What are the key things that will enable this to be established permanently and not just experienced in a moment? We do well to ask these questions, due to the great difference between our transient experiences and the kingdom established.

Remember of course, I'm not claiming to have all the answers here, but I will share a few thoughts.

Jesus gives us a clue as He continues in prayer:

"I have given to them the glory and honour which you have given Me, that they may be one as We are one: I in them and You in me, in order that they may become one and perfectly united, that the world may know and recognize that You sent Me and that You have loved them as You have loved me."

Jn.17:22-23

Jesus says He has given us His glory that we may be one. What does that mean?

Not to take the glory and presence of God as being equivocal, but we know very well the profound and powerful unity that the presence of God brings. Not least because in His presence our hearts become so flooded with His love we want to hug everything that moves! With all hearts gazing heavenwards, we cannot fail to see His likeness in each other. Furthermore, His presence notably expands when united we stand. We find effortless union in the convergence of deep drinkers: coming together from a deep place of prayer, already full of the presence of the Lord and walking in union.

I will take a short digression:

A long time ago the Lord started speaking to me about the meaning of true fellowship and unity, and how we can create it amongst ourselves.

"But if we really are living and walking in the Light as He Himself is in the light, we have true, unbroken fellowship with one another, and the blood of Jesus Christ His Son cleanses us from all sin and guilt"

1 John 1:7

If we walk in the light we have true, unbroken fellowship.

I have noticed a dynamic which occurs when we meet people of kindred spirit: the ease of connection we experience may cause us to feel as if we've known each other for years. We share the unity of the Spirit and the fellowship of the presence of God – this is why. We have been walking in the light, and by this we find effortless fellowship in the harmony of God. If we take *the light* here as the light of the presence of the Lord, we begin to understand this experience. We have every encouragement in this to dive into God's presence and embrace the unity that springs up from it!

For a time I studied 'unity' throughout the New Testament, and I happened upon an interesting discovery: the great majority of the time that unity is mentioned, it is described as *the unity of the Spirit*, not simply unity. This is an important distinction. Only the Holy Spirit can create the unity of God in us; it is a spiritual thing, we cannot create it by the efforts of man. In addition, we find that in the presence of God: His glory unites us in a transcendent way – it goes way beyond what we can do ourselves, we even feel the spiritual substance of oneness!

The future truly is ecumenical

Many of the unifying strategies attempted by the people of God in the past, have been our own plans and efforts – uniting not in spirit, but trying to unite in doctrine, organization etc., sadly we can see how little fruit this brings. We can only go so far absent His unifying love drawing us together. I consider it a great blessing to have seen some really special and successful projects where the unity of God has prevailed amongst a truly diverse group of believers – the future truly is ecumenical. Let us not forget: the harmony God is seeking to establish is by no means monochrome; we are made to be an eclectic mish-mash of beautiful lovers intertwined on this spiritual journey and as our paths cross we hold hands and dive further in: loving our differences, helping each other, putting each other first, seeing this great glory of Christ in each one expressed uniquely!

I would struggle to think of a sweeter vision to carry than *the unity of God fully manifest in us,* just the thought of it excites my heart so much. When talking to people all across the British Isles, almost everyone responds to this deep desire for community and fellowship and so few seem to have found anything close at the present time. So my prayer is simple, *reveal Your glory, make us one, do what only You can!*

I have a final point, coming back to the prayer of Jesus:

"I have given to them the glory and honour which you have given Me, that they may be one as We are one: I in them and You in me, in order that they may become one and perfectly united, that the world may know and recognize that You sent Me and that You have loved them as You have loved me."

Jn.17:22-23

The last thing He says is quite profound:

"...that the world may know... that You have loved them as You have loved me."

Somehow, Jesus is implying that *His glory in us* and *His unity in us, will reveal His love to all the world.* Our loving each other will open the eyes of people to the Father's love for the Son – and that *we are all loved by Him in this same way.* The power of this is so great that I am often surprised at how distracted some folks are – focusing on the finer details of doctrine, when *if we simply learn to love: the world will be turned upside down again!*

Do me a favour:

Ask me if I'm growing in love

If I say yes, but you don't feel it

Tell me

The natural state of a follower of Jesus
is to be an outpouring of love

Our unity is brewing in the heart of the father

United Hearts, One Voice

"Finally, all [of you] should be of one and the same mind [united in spirit], sympathizing [with one another], loving [each other] as brethren [of one household], compassionate and courteous (tenderhearted and humble)."

1 Pet.3:8

"But concerning brotherly love, you have no need to have anyone write you, for you yourselves have been [personally] taught by God to love one another. And indeed you already are [extending and displaying your love] to all the brethren throughout Macedonia. But we beseech and earnestly exhort you, brethren, that you excel [in this matter] more and more."

1 Thes.4:9-10*

Paul could see that God had taught the Thessalonians to love each other – without any man teaching them how or what it would look like. Without exception, we see a lot of love displayed in the lives of those who are mature in Christ. This profound experience is one that is worthy of our attention, since it demonstrates and witnesses to the truths that John teaches in his first letter – that those who obey and follow God walk in love, and that God will teach us to love if ever we will walk with Him. For us to *know God* and not find Him teaching us the way of love would be strange to say the least...

"Now may the God who gives the power of patient endurance (steadfastness) and Who supplies encouragement, grant you to live in such mutual harmony and such full sympathy with one another, in accord with Christ Jesus, That together you may [unanimously] with united hearts and one voice, praise and glorify the God and Father of our Lord Jesus Christ (the Messiah). Welcome and receive [to your hearts] one another, then, even as Christ has welcomed and received you, for the glory of God."

Rom.15:5-7

There is so much in this! Maybe it speaks for itself?!

"But I urge and entreat you, brethren, by the name of our Lord Jesus Christ, that all of you be in perfect harmony and full agreement in what you say, and that there be no dissensions or factions or divisions among you, but that you be perfectly united in your common understanding and in your opinions and judgements."

1 Cor.1:10

This is a considerable mystery! Our path to finding this level of oneness and communion is found in our embracing love as our central purpose. As we noted before, love discerns what is of real value and so both preferring one another and embracing true wisdom, we will choose our battles carefully and only contend when we feel compelled by love. God has given us an unbreakable promise that He will give us one heart (Jer.32:39); this is found in a heart devoted to God - the *unity of the Spirit* is found by our uniting first with God, and by so doing we will find ourselves united with one another.

Romantic love throws preferences out of the window,

Shouldn't brotherly love work the same way?

Tribes & Structures

One of the primary drivers that divided us in the past is our commitment to doctrine, often at the expense of love. There is a day coming when our ideals and value systems harmonize with His on a greater level, and they are no longer the *dividing lines of the tribes.* Our culture is already changing and people are learning to stand together regardless of strong doctrinal differences. When all the separate streams come into the revelation of love as *the main thing* and commit to loving, we will find ourselves beautifully unified.

God teaches us not only to embrace diversity, but truly to love it, to see Him working in all of it (1 Cor.12:5-6). The love of diversity disarms the clash of value systems. We even grow to love all the ways Jesus works – especially those which are not our defaults. What would Jesus say in regard to *the love languages* or *personality profiles* we have developed? – Who knows? (except perhaps to acknowledge the impact they have achieved in helping people understand each other a little better). These tools are not *just* useful reference frames for understanding one another and communicating better; but can function as invitations to explore life and break out of our own walls, allowing our hearts to evolve. We are not static people, and neither are our ideas or perspectives. Adventuring into alternative perspectives on life can help us understand others no end, *spend ten minutes in their shoes...*

One of the great riches of maturity is the growth of our weaker areas; our becoming well rounded, rising above the usual paradigms and embracing our opposites: exploring activities and perspectives that we find unnatural, this can be in fact profoundly liberating. We find that this maturity of perspective sees the worth in everything and the strengths in all the various approaches. We see how each perspective on a given spectrum has its valid place: the time when it is most useful. In this process we also observe the optimums: which perspectives are most broadly useful (all cultures are not created equal, for example). Those who always seek to learn (a natural perspective of humility – *Get wisdom!)* will find this path most easily. We can learn also to love in all these diverse ways. I view it similarly to the gifts of the Spirit: we may have particular gifts that we exercise with greater success or more natural ability; but the Holy Spirit who carries all the gifts lives in us all. If we value each other highly enough we will desire to connect, to empathise, to find common ground and to meet people on their level. We cannot retain a public expression of all our niche preferences and reach the state of full harmony in God. We will gladly lay these down for our friends; holding our passions lightly and pointing first and foremost to the big picture...

What is the result then? That in the end, love is no longer looking at the weaknesses and failings of other people, cultures and streams; but simply celebrating their strengths and holding their hands high calling them on into the more, glorifying God for all that He does!

God has set us on a course to disarm all that stands between us:

We undertake: to never again build walls between our brothers

To not focus on things that divide us

And to seize all opportunities for love.

The notion of our being *one body* (Rom.12:5), supersedes the idea of *tribes*, yet so often we cling first to our church structures. A kingdom culture has dawned where people view all things in terms of relationships before structures: a *relational revolution* as it were; this perspective is more accurate, a greater truth and as such we cannot return to the old ways.

Paul was deeply concerned at the immaturity of the Corinthians (1 Cor.3), who were behaving like *'mere infants;'* perhaps a similar situation as we find described in the letter to the Hebrews – who ought to have been teachers by this time (Heb.5:12). Paul cites the presence of factions and divisions as primary signs of a deep immaturity. The comparisons we make between each other are considered *unwise* at best (2 Cor.10:12): all are given different graces, all have different callings and all are created unique, it is clearly futile! He laments their factions – *all are of Christ!* Does it matter who our favourite teachers are?!

"Do NOTHING from factional motives or prompted by conceit and empty arrogance..."

Rom.12:16, emphasis added

In Christ we are all *in Jesus* before we are part of any tribe and Christ is our head (Col.1:18); so why is there such great concern about which tribe people are a part of; defining, boxing and stereotyping a believer by their current associations, and judging them by assumptions regarding their apparent theological reference frame? Are we not to welcome each other in the true Spirit of Christ with open arms? (Rom.15:7) And how is there not more interest in learning from other tribes and working collaboratively? Surely the sense of belonging that we long to find in tribes should be found in belonging to Christ and in connecting with the family in whatever way – is there a way to find this with any believer?! After all, we have so much in common! (Eph.4:4-6) We have one and the same Spirit, the same Lord and Father, the same faith and hope!

Love will expose the folly of divisions and undo them entirely

"...for as long as [there are] envying and jealousy and wrangling and factions among you, are you not unspiritual and of the flesh, behaving yourselves after a human standard and like mere (unchanged) men? For when one says, I belong to Paul, and another, I belong to Apollos, are you not [proving yourselves] ordinary (unchanged) men?"

1 Cor.3:3-5

– We all belong to Jesus –

Let no one exult proudly concerning men, for all things are yours
1 Cor.3:21-23

All the people of God belong to us all

Paul carried a heart for all the believers and for all the churches, even all men: this is the spirit of a true father.

Why am I saying all this? My desire is that all the brethren would love one another, and that an end to divisions between the various groups will come. I want for the saints to be free to follow natural relationships, and where God is cultivating connections between the streams; to not feel the need for man's permissions to pursue these when God has given a clear call to His disciples. Many of the glorious plans of God will only be completely fulfilled in our working together, and such collaboration is a humility that He has designed into our circumstances. The kingdom of God exists regardless of all our structures and programs, and whilst they may be helpful, it is a great benefit for us to see the kingdom as it is – in the spirit, *as God sees it*. My point is simply this, the walls between peoples and tribes do not exist, they are only perceived, and God sees the true substance in our lives regardless of our structures. He sees those who genuinely carry spiritual authority and He sees those who are self appointed, regardless of what men say is true. Heavenly realities and spiritual truths take precedent over earthly realities. I long for the day when brothers celebrate all the tribes together and even long to be part of all God is doing elsewhere, not repelled by theological divisions and offences of the past. In the same way that men have become too focused on their ministries – even exalted them above the love of Christ Himself, *churches* have been exalted above the love, fellowship and truth of union in God. If we have become so narrowly focused on our own tribe and family, that we are not very aware of what God is doing elsewhere, is this not an extension of an excessive self-focus expressed in a collective sphere? *The culture and Spirit of Christ is the same – whether we apply it on an individual or corporate level.*

Are we truly serving Jesus?
or are we building our own churches and ministries?

A greater harmony is established when we focus on Jesus over church and theology. We can lead each other into deeper union with Him by keeping the focus on Him and by looking for points of common connection and experience. (– Rather than debate theology, which so often follows a predictable route causing us to distance ourselves from one another... is this because knowledge puffs up? (1 Cor.8:1) Or have we fallen pray to the vain and empty discussions we have been warned to avoid (1 Tim.1:6, 6:4, 2 Tim.2:23.)) We can share testimonies and histories – so that we have an appreciation of each one's emotional and spiritual journey – a connection over experience can be considerably easier to find than over theology. We are in the process of being rewired and becoming well balanced, finally shaking off the Western predisposition to 'only logic' which can be so unfruitful. The scholar's error has always been to focus too much on the little things that are not of great import, no wonder the great majority can find it so difficult to connect with the scholar – he does not rightly divide the truth and appreciate the relative weight and (lack of) importance in his small ideas in light of the grand scheme! This is the error of the Pharisees! – To focus on the finer points of doctrine (or sometimes in our case – church details,) without the love *which is its very purpose*... How much greater are the practical needs of the people than the need to search out these finest conceptual details? **The essential truths are as clear as day and are not the focus of any great debate!**

How much agreement do we look for
before we are prepared to work with one another?

I want to ask all my brothers and sisters to consider how Jesus views us? How does He view our institutions, and how He views our relationships?

What does He see?

– one new man –

Eph.2:15

Every kingdom divided against itself is brought to desolation (Mt.12:25), division is a direct blockage to the kingdom of God, wherever and to whatever degree it is manifest. The heart to unify the body and create harmony is one which is growing amongst God's people; if we are to be the solution, how best can we do this? We know that a large proportion of the failings in the church in recent decades have been due to dysfunctional relationships. We should therefore attempt to master this field and become a generation who develop heavenly relationships, leaving no room open for our enemy! (2 Cor.2:10-11) Knowing that our primary mission in life is to love; it is remarkable that in past times God's people have not prioritised training in relational skills...

The heart to unify the body is growing amongst God's people

We are the true temple of God: *people.* People and relationships are the structure of the actual temple of God in the spirit. This spiritual truth supersedes the earthly temporal structures. I cannot get away from this truth! It is people and not *cells* or anything else that are the building blocks of the Church. The kingdom of God is built by building up people! And I love that this puts the focus back on *everyone* and not just *leaders or forms.* This is partly why pursuing natural relationships and connections with people is something we should do freely and is something not to be frowned upon.

"We put no obstruction in anybodies way"

2 Cor.6:3

When the Lord was re-gauging my perspective on fellowship (a number of years ago), the first thing He pointed to was the life – *where is the life of God? – in what relationships?* Relationships are the primary structure God uses for the spreading of life and this will never change. As regards our lofty ideas about wineskins, I have to wonder how much of our desire to rethink it all could just be a vain distraction... and will the Lord bless it, if we are putting less effort into growing our relationships and making them work – the real essence of life and the essential ingredient? Have we not seen moves of God amid all kinds of structures and is this not the essence of this message – God and people are the focus and the key to it all, not the form or structure?

> *How can we be interested in how great the wineskin is*
>
> *if there is no wine?!*

Nature teaches us that the purpose of structure is to enable life to flourish, it is there to facilitate it, but is not designed to constrain it. I have long taken the view, that if our structures are not benefiting us or fulfilling their purpose, we ought to be rid of them! As we proceed into these coming decades, and with much discussion on the future of fellowship: consideration of new wine skins, attempts to restore a more monastic way of life, *fresh expressions* etc.; let us not forget that *restructuring cannot bring us a move of God.* I sincerely hope that we can learn this the easy way, rather than throwing our energies into pursuing fruitless experiments. It is suffice to say, *God alone is the magic bullet.* (And I am in no way intending to discourage folks from restructuring under the direction of God, but to see it for what it is...)

- God is the magic bullet -

One of the motivations behind the recent *deconstruction movement* was to see the true heart unveiled through stripping back our organisations (I am not commenting here on my general thoughts on this). There certainly can be a place for breaking down to find the roots and foundations and in so doing, exposing the heart. God took me through a season years ago where He challenged me regarding where my faith was really at: If all the support structures around me were removed, what would happen? If our churches were closed down by the state, our families and friends deserted Christ, how strong were my foundations? Would I still follow Jesus if the world around me fell apart? His purpose was to cultivate in me a deep personal spirituality that would stand the test no matter what trials come, and for sure they will come. I sincerely believe this is actually a really beneficial experience for every believer to go through: to recognize where we find life and to see how valuable it is to strengthen our foundations and really get to know God personally. In my experience this journey is not so much about dissociation from fellowship for a time; but rather pursuing God one on one and finding Him on such a depth as to walk in the power of God.

If all the structures and support were stripped away,

What would our walk with God look like?

Standing on the principle spiritual truths of our union with one another, with Christ at the head: from this place – the relational perspective, we cannot go back to an institutional paradigm. When we see the greater principle, the fuller, deeper and more complete understanding, we can never deny it – *the old boxes are broken forever*. To use a colloquial idea, it's like asking a quantum physicist to work in the classical paradigm... (The cat lives!) Or to use a spiritual analogy, it is like asking someone who lives in the spiritual freedom of sonship to go back to a driven, works based regime, we cannot do it!

We are the temple of God!

Acts of Fellowship

"Fill up and complete my joy by living in harmony and being of the same mind and one in purpose, having the same love, being in full accord and of one harmonious mind and intention."

Phil.2:2

Having *the same love? – Reciprocal Relationships!*

His joy is complete:

when the community walks together harmoniously

He wants this Holy Spirit community more than we do!

The fellowship we read about early on in the book of Acts is one that has inspired so many (Acts 2:42-47, 4:32-25). The source of this expression of fellowship was *the fruit of the Spirit*. If we attempt to recreate the natural community dynamics they had, without finding the source of it, we fall short. Why did they freely share all they had and sell their possessions for the good of the many? I don't believe that it was simply the Apostles command, Peter even indicated to Ananias – they really didn't have to sell up (Acts 5:4). It seems most probable that the love of the Spirit in the hearts of these early disciples lead them to pledge both their possessions, their time – even their very lives to one another. Perhaps they were actually living according to Jesus' teachings on the kingdom of God?

"Let your love be sincere..."

Rom.12:9

- He has made us comrades in arms forevermore -

Community: from the joining of *common* and *unity,* similar to communion: from *common* and *union.* Communities often function around *common spaces*, both private and public. If we first consider the wider spheres of society: the loss of *the commons* – public spaces, places of free assembly and conversation – to corporate control, it is a current concern for a significant proportion of the populace. It is also generally true, that where collectives no longer have a great deal in common they will struggle to unify in a substantial way. With the expansion of culture into a thousand niche worlds, it will take a much greater determination to bring us all back together, a heavenly dimension perhaps? Nonetheless, the desire for community is almost so ubiquitous one could legitimately suggest – *community is on everyone's mind;* some even think of it almost nostalgically, as though the soul of the nation has withered away amidst technological advances and convenience services. I wonder if our desiring heavenly community is an expression of us *seeking a homeland* (Heb.11:16). We love the concept and romanticise about it so often – like *the good old days*, a perfect childhood or a fairytale marriage. True it is *such a valuable treasure,* and what a noble ideal to meditate upon and hunger for! It is even more curious then that our ideas of community can look so different in all our respective fantasy lands! And how come we haven't made more progress down this road to date? How much is due to progression in modern culture, greater independence, and the life choices we make? I suppose if we consider the competing factors which have stood between us and a bona fide community lifestyle, this is no small battle. Our time is extremely precious; we are a busy people, highly committed to both work and family. And beyond this, the matters of spiritual calling, our personal walk with Jesus and the various long term projects He has called us to. Do we realistically have the time to raise up a family and do all this, while living in community?

So what does the Holy Spirit say about all this? What is to be our focus? I genuinely believe He wants to be the focus – not the community, He will hold it together. It is not in our embracing a method or way of seeking him, not simply the beautiful union of friends, but of His Spirit and presence, *for in my presence the people understand love and find true union and fruitfulness.* He is also seeking to establish *houses of grace:* that extend His very grace to one another and houses of fellowship, bringing healing to the body of Christ and enabling many who could not heal to come home again. I do not wish to keep making the point, but when we come to the place of valuing *each other* over whatever else we are preoccupied with, somehow by God's grace, all the world will stand under one roof. Surely this could never happen absent the love of Christ?!

"Love one another with brotherly affection, giving precedence and showing honour to one another"

Rom.12:10

Family

God desires to dwell with a family on the earth, a community in which all the generations are valued and included. A people who treat their spiritual family: brothers and sisters in Christ as their very own. We recognise that we are joined to them as one in spirit, whatever affects them affects us (1 Cor.12:26) – and not just because we are joined in theory, but in heart. We all love the idea of living in community, but I genuinely believe the kind of community the Spirit of God wants to build amongst us is a family one. The family culture gives us a number of key reference points for how God desires

His heart to be expressed through us; these are particularly helpful and perhaps not as self evident in alternative community structures.

"And if one member suffers, all the parts [share] the suffering; if one member is honoured, all the members [share in] the enjoyment of it."

1 Cor.12:26

The Spirit of adoption is seeking to adopt people into His family through us, literally sweeping them into a sense of *home and belonging*. People love to be embraced as a part of a wider family and we know what great lengths people will go to in order to belong. How much more glorious for them, when their belonging is no longer dependent on their performance, but acceptance is freely offered?!

"Let love for your fellow believers continue and be a fixed practice with you [never let it fail]."

Heb.13:1

A family makes place for all the various levels of maturity to be present – in flexibility catering for each one and therefore often prioritising the young. It operates in an inclusive manner and all things are shared in common. Perhaps we need only ask ourselves the question - *what would we do for our natural relatives?*

"Contribute to the needs of God's people; pursue the practice of hospitality."

Rom.12:13*

"Let all men know your unselfishness"

Phil.4:5

Practically speaking, we are called to *"readily adjust yourselves to people,"* to *"give yourselves to humble tasks"* and to *"never overestimate yourself or be wise in your own conceits" (Rom.12:16)*. If anyone ever comes to think of themselves of being above humble tasks, and serving others, they have lost the spirit of Christ! So in this we have every case to ask all of our brothers in community to fulfil their practical duties, to keep our houses clean and tidy and for *all* to pull their weight. We desire to treat our guests with the utmost honour, and as such our homes should reflect this!

The Five Fold Role

"And His gifts were [varied; He Himself appointed and gave men to us] some to be apostles, some to be prophets, some evangelists, some pastors and teachers. His intention was the perfecting and the full equipping of the saints, [that they should do] the work of ministering toward building up Christ's body, [That it might develop] until we all attain oneness in the faith and in the comprehension of the [full and accurate] knowledge of the Son of God, that [we might arrive] at really mature manhood, the measure of the stature of the fullness of the Christ and the completeness found in Him."

Eph.4:11-13*

The five fold ministry is given as a gift from God that the saints might be equipped for this service: to build up the body of Christ in love, until it reaches *oneness in the faith* (i.e. unity) and full maturity. The giving of love is integral to our coming to completeness in Christ and always contributes to our being built up into His nature (**v16**). The focus is clearly on the work of the body, the five fold ministries simply helping (equipping) the people to accomplish the work of the kingdom.

If the believers are equipped and working effectively to build up the body in love, and have come to a place of maturity and oneness in Christ, then what of the role of the five fold in relation to these? (I'm only asking the question...)

The five fold ministry exists to draw us into unity and maturity

– Leadership in the Great Covenant –

"Behold, I am doing a new thing! Now it springs forth"

Is.43:19

We have explored some of the fundamental principles that underpin the nature of authentic Christ-like leadership. There are so many open questions that remain. As much as I would love to examine them all in order to develop a thoroughly comprehensive and holistic set of conclusions; a full discussion of leadership styles and perspectives is clearly beyond the scope of this book. That said, the examination of family and community dynamics we have undertaken stands somewhat incomplete, absent a little further consideration.

I have included this section therefore to elaborate further, to introduce additional fresh ideas so that the profound implications of our true spiritual unity and freedom find a deeper measure of completion. Whilst carrying substantial validity, some of what I propose is not often considered in traditional circles and in part serves as a counterweight to the views of the established church. Many of the concepts we consider here are simply a collection of alternative perspectives which are naturally born out of asking genuine questions of the scriptures, and gleaning from the wisdom of our experiences. The courage to ask questions should not be suppressed.

Led by the Spirit

God is calling us into deeper communion with one another. A growing company of people have stumbled upon an awareness that God is seeking to shake things up, to bring forth genuine fresh expressions; He has purposed to build His family to express love more completely in the earth. Many of us have been led into seasons of exploration in which the heartbeat is the question – *where is the life?* In this context, groups of leaders are experiencing revelations of the big picture and determining to walk together, *the time for cooperative leadership has arrived.* Not only this, but as God is building maturity into His people, we can now recognise the validity of mature sons walking with God, without the need for hierarchical oversight. God is revealing to us biblically based holistic alternatives for how we do life as communities. We have found great life in natural, decentralised networks of friendship – so much life that it prompted a full back to basics look at our ideas about the church (as discussed in the above chapters). As the present spiritual revolution continues; with the saints empowered through discovering their union with God, with the depths of spirituality open wide to all, and as we see the kingdom of God come – questions about leadership, organisations and communities will come to the forefront. How should an empowered community led by the Holy Spirit operate? What role do we have to play as leaders? What if *God* can lead us?

How should an empowered community
led by the Holy Spirit operate?

How can we sing: (in faith)

"Set a fire down in my soul, that I can't contain, that I can't control"

United Pursuit Band

– And not anticipate a move of God that looks like this?

Without a doubt we must confront the spirit of religion. We could almost define the spirit of religion as *"a form of godliness without power"* (2 Tim.3:5). In the record we have of Jesus life, he confronted and challenged the religious directly more than any other group. That which masquerades as God can be the most deceptive of all (Mt.23:27). We find this religion caught up in powerless, rigid forms – hence taking the time here to consider the structures and forms our organisations are based on. There is frequently a partnership between the spirit of religion and the systems of man, so perhaps we need ask ourselves again – *have we embraced powerless forms?*

It is high time to shake off every powerless form of godliness

Our theology of leadership is a key aspect of this discussion; this is necessary as our expectations of the role of the Holy Spirit and His relationship with His people are paramount. This is clearly not just about love, but about His Lordship. We find ourselves asking – have we submitted to God? And more specifically (as leaders), have we submitted whatever we believe He has given us responsibility for to Him – His people, His church, the ways and means, our methods and ideas, timings and expectations – even all the things we are leading? Do we recognise His leadership? How does He want to lead us? How much input do we anticipate from Him and through whom will it come? Will He lead us completely, i.e. give us a full blueprint of His plans? So when I ask the question – *do we truly trust Him?* This connects directly to our submission of all this to Him. Perhaps we should consider the model of Jesus, Whom we are following, in the same vein (Jn.20:21, 1 Jn.4:17, Jn.14:12); He did nothing that He did not see or hear the Father doing! He could do nothing else... (Jn.5:19-20, 30)

The absence of input from the Holy Spirit, whether it be in the form of prophetic insights, highlighting of scripture or Him prompting our conscience, will make us reliant on our own ideas and strategies. We can maintain *forms of godliness* without power and His intervention, but certainly not the other way round. In the midst of this absence, men are attempting to stand in His place and take His job – to strategise, substitute our own ideas for His voice and attempt to release the kingdom without His direct involvement. That which is born of the flesh is flesh and that which is born of the spirit is spirit, we cannot manufacture anything of substance ourselves (Jn.3:6). We are a spiritual people and we must operate from spiritual insight and power. By attempting to cut out the very thing He seeks – relationship with us and with His people – to attempt to operate without His input is one of the greatest of follies imaginable. If we try to manage without Him, how are we surprised when we do not experience His presence? Or when our efforts are fruitless? To embrace these truths leaves us desperately reliant on God, but this is only daunting to those who do not really know Him and His guarantee of releasing the kingdom! (He simply wishes to do it with us, in His way...)

He absolutely loves releasing the kingdom!

(Lk.12:32)

One of the first things (recorded), Jesus pledged to His disciples is:

"I will make you fishers of men."

Mt.4:19, NASB

The coming of the kingdom

Is the most natural experience for followers of Jesus

A Community of Equals

Our viewpoints on leadership *must* take into consideration what God has established in the New Covenant (Heb.8:10-13!) – Christ alone is our mediator and He is the only head of the true Church (1 Tim.2:5, Eph.1:22). We no longer have men, priests, 'leaders' *between* us and God: we are now *all* both kings and priests in the heavenly order! (1 Pet.2:9) *There is no two tier system in the kingdom!* No more division between an elevated elite priesthood and 'lesser' servant saints or any such nonsense! (Mt.23:8) Such is abhorrent to the blood of Christ and should be as far away from our culture as possible. We are now one with God and one with the whole body of Christ! We have *equality* before God. This Great Covenant constitutes a full spectrum paradigm shift! Of course, leadership does not cease to exist in this Covenant, but it takes on the form of Jesus – influence, inspiration and example, rather than positional or hierarchical. Old Covenant models of leadership are dead and gone – He takes away the first to establish the second – He makes the first one Obsolete! (Heb.10:9, 8:13) We have *heroes not celebrities*, and these heroes are the most ordinary people of all living in faith before God. Even submission to leadership is now counterbalanced by submission to one another (Heb.13:17, Eph.5:21), and should *always* bring life. As I suggested previously, this notion of submit is *common sense* – to listen to and follow the advice of the wise – *if* they are truly wise and have our best interests at heart. We are always free to disagree, and to determine what we believe. The call to hope in all things and believe the best of others is not a call to be naive and gullible, or to follow blind immature 'leaders' ignoring the truth before our very eyes! Jesus instructed us to be *"wise as serpents!" (Mt.10:16)* Let us always remember – *the individual is the one who carries the most responsibility for their own life and decisions before God, their conscience must therefore be respected;* so If God speaks to us, we must obey Him! (Heb.3:7-8, despite the complication of *resolving differences of conviction* this can bring.)

"And it will nevermore be necessary for each one to teach his neighbour and his fellow citizen or each one his brother, saying Know (perceive, have knowledge of, and get acquainted by experience with) the Lord, for all will know Me, from the smallest to the greatest of them."

Heb.8:11

We are the believer priesthood.

We are His kings.

True Authority

The source of the purest form of authority is love, (and in a sense true relationship). Regardless of the sphere or extent of responsibility, love should always be the basis. There is a spiritual authority carried by those who love God – His very friends; we see this authority in the lives of true fathers. There is no need to justify the authority that is always present with love, and we can see its spiritual substance; it is further validated by peoples' willingness to yield to it. Love permissions the greatest authority in any individual's life and forms the foundation which enables vulnerability. When we see the heart of a servant, we identify one we can trust, for service proves love and trust to others. We have seen so many times how a heart operating in love can say things that no one else can ever say, and so can bring the greatest challenges – people receiving them can actually hear and embrace them without the offence that would otherwise occur. When we find those who stand in love, we long to develop relationships with them, to draw on their advice, to open up – there is no need to ask people to open up to you – all they need to see is your love for them. People are longing to connect if only they can find a safe place, and so by loving we draw out their hearts. In this sense this love will empower the gospel, for we can deliver it in this spirit and people will be able to receive it who otherwise would have been hardened to it.

We do well to consider whether our authority structures and theology are rooted deep in love - trust, mutual respect and honour, grace and peace. If love is not the foundation of all that we are doing, we have no legitimate basis from which to lead anyone in the kingdom of God. The value of every individual is far greater than the value of church structures and policies – the structure is for the people, not the people for the structure! (Mk.2:27) Even those communities that have disbanded or decentralised their structures will not function well without a deep understanding of how to cultivate healthy relationships – it is not simply a case of finding the best form. Furthermore, hierarchical systems stand in questionable legitimacy both in the world and the kingdom of God – *Jesus taught the opposite!* We are *never* to laud it *over* one another (Mt.20:25-26). Top-down systems notoriously de-value people and fail to release them into their full potential. I hold it self-evident that an environment of love will be empowering, and will not in any way disenfranchise, oppress or control people. Any theology that is born out of immaturity, insecurities, or more specifically – fear, pride (and the like), is one which will only bear bad fruit. Surely the desire to control others comes only from fear, a lack of trust in God or man, or pride? The end of competition and elitism, hypocrisy and double standards, coercion and manipulation, suspicion and fear is long overdue, *God help us!*

*"For wherever there is jealousy and contention
there will also be confusion and all sorts of evil and vile practises."*

Jam.3:16*

- Pure authority is based on love -

Whilst the focus of love may not be as clearly expressed in this discourse on organisational structures, leadership and group dynamics; the essential connection to the theme can be seen through the lens of a collection of questions, as follows: Do our theology, leadership and organisational frameworks produce a culture which is entirely conducive to love? Are the saints valued and respected for who they are within our communities? Do they have a voice? Do we know each other well? (This is a really crucial point – people need to be known to feel valued, *and Pr.27:23*.) Do the people have roles that accurately fit them? Are they empowered in the full pursuit of their destiny and the release of their gifts? (Do we know how to do this? – Or is our culture centred on particular powerful figures? Or worse - do saints have to qualify themselves through new systems of law before they are considered 'safe' to work for God*?!)* Are the saints controlled in any way or free under God? Do any of our theological or structural frameworks stand in the way of the Spirit of God or make us resistant to His moving? (So for example, if God starts moving in a way we have not seen before, do not understand, and with people we do not know – how do we respond?) Have our structures and theology become a law to us, a stumbling block or pretext for the spirit of religion? (2 Cor.3:6)

One of the most unloving things we can do is stand in the way of God's work in someone's life, or hold people back from their destinies; hence the need for us to consider these issues. It is a fundamental principle of love to discover and acknowledge who someone truly is; this should clearly be an early priority in new relationships. My desire is for *all the saints* to recognise their value, their gifts and the callings of God on their lives, and henceforth pursue Him and live them out – not restrained by the hindrance of unnecessary official structures, hoops of legalism and 'leaders' *so-called*.

Practical Submission

The submission we are called to is relatively pragmatic and contextual, it is always voluntary, never absolute (except to God) and it is not a new law! By contextual I mean: in every sphere of life there are leaders – those who are responsible for the organisation and management of what happens in any given endeavour. Whilst engaged in these endeavours (e.g. within church activities), someone needs to take the final decision on things, even if we adopt a relatively democratic structure. Here we draw the patently clear observation – if we are fighting against people leading projects we are involved in, we are working against ourselves – and potentially God – *and* we will never get anything done! – Aside from the fact that we are missing the point (Mt.12:25), we should choose our battles well. The overarching principle here is that for any organisation to function well: people need to submit to a degree to its aims and methods – no less true of a church *organisation*. Leaders are appointed a jurisdiction of responsibility: this alone is what they have authority over; their authority does not therefore extend to areas beyond this jurisdiction, to our workplaces for example.

For the sake of completeness, we will look briefly at that which Peter taught regarding submission to human authority *for the sake of the Lord* (1 Pet.2:13). First of all, his primary example is the authority of the State. In both biblical references that encourage us to submit to it, the role of the State is cited – *to uphold security and justice*. Recall the above paragraph, if we do not submit to a degree to the State it cannot function in this role. The full subject of States and their administration of justice (or otherwise) will be left for another time. The reasons Peter gives here for submission come under the upside-down principles of the kingdom: choosing to adopt the Christ-like position of humility – a shining faultless example: in order that we bring glory to God, silencing our enemies through our good conduct, (the only quarrel people are to find with us is over our faith). The kingdom *belongs* to the humble (Mt.5:3). God is clearly looking to form the character of Christ in us; the willingness and readiness to submit in humility to whatever God may bring our way, holding our own ideas lightly. Our zeal and love for God alone (not our own desires or rebellion,) are the basis and cause for us to speak out, to object and if the need arises to follow a different course. God is looking for our full obedience and often seems to work through these circumstances: the little injustices, inconveniences. There is no less a clear need to discern when it is appropriate to submit or otherwise. The lack of wisdom in choosing our battles: by not considering the wider repercussions and affects on the community before standing against authority structures, has inadvertently resulted in unnecessary community splits, discord and a great deal of pain. It is a sober calling to oppose people. One final thought on this – apparently God saw fit to sneak *"live as free people"* (v16) into the middle of this discourse on submission, landing us with a classic scriptural duality...

There are a few further beliefs regarding leadership theology and submission which are often held, but find no place within a New Covenant framework. Firstly and fundamentally, we cannot equate the church with the kingdom of God; this misappropriation provides the foundation for the most common of theological faux pas. Other writers have covered this subject extensively, highlighting the nature of the distinctions and I feel no necessity to substantiate this point again. We see these faux pas manifest in a number of forms though, for example – to always equate *submission* to church 'leadership,' as submission to God is a clear step too far and has been used as a pretext for all manner of ungodly things! (*The Church is not an institution! Spiritual realities are distinct from and supersede earthly frameworks. The true Church is a spiritual temple made up only of people. Position in church does not equate to maturity, neither does maturity infer institutional 'position' should be pursued. We can be spiritual leaders without position.*) The assumption implies that leaders are always right and are in essence the voice of God, (oh that this were true!) And that God would never call His people to contradict the line a leader chooses to take. Some have perverted this idea even further to suggest that if we are not submitted directly to *the organised church*, we are not submitted to God and therefore have left ourselves open and vulnerable to the attacks of the enemy. What a peculiar controlling manifestation of the spirit of religion! It is Jesus alone, His blood, being seated with Him in the heavens (by grace through faith) – and the like, which guards us spiritually and keeps us safe. The truth is: these traditional ideas are based on a lack of trust in God, by practice we are saying we trust men to look after us more than the Holy Spirit.

The kingdom of God and the church are not equivalent

Prophetic Rebels

Some have gone so far as to believe that we cannot fulfil our callings or make spiritual progress without this 'submission' to the organised church. History appears to tell a profoundly different story. If we take the great history of the saints and how they walked before God, together with our own experience and the potential that the Word of God says is possible, we cannot believe such nonsense.

So what do we make of John the Baptist and Jesus? They were *prophetic rebels!* – Cutting a new way and leading expanding movements separate from and uncontained by the synagogues, respectively. What of those who were slung out of the synagogues for believing in Jesus? *And* all this time Jesus was walking and leading in love. (Apparently in His case this is what love looked like). So in reflection, do we judge people now for not fitting into traditional styles of Christian gatherings? Or judge them for not adopting a lifestyle and rhythm that we understand? Do we accept that God calls people to walk differently? – We must walk in the way God has called us; not emulating another if we are not called to live in the way they do (like someone else trying to be John the Baptist, God is *not* calling us to be clones!)

To take this thesis one step further, which of the great acts of faith recorded and given to us for our instruction were called for and sanctioned first by the church? Which of the prophets did they receive? And in more recent years, which of the moves of the Spirit and His messengers were received by the traditional churches at the time? Many were slung out! They had to start over, start something new, they were persecuted by their spiritual family; yet in the midst of all this determined to *do whatever it takes to obey God*. This incredible *'I will not be stopped by anything'* heartbeat prevailed: my food is to do His will. Of course, as history shows us all too well, after death they are later received and welcomed as heroes. The warning of Jesus springs to mind – *"woe to you when all men speak well of you, for their fathers used to treat the false prophets in the same way"* (Lk.6:26). Maybe we can learn to receive God's messengers while they are alive?! I also wonder if the greats of old, these time honoured spiritual entrepreneurs, had waited for men to 'release them,' or similarly had attempted to keep the 'authorities' of the day happy (!) – *Would we have had any revival at all?* I have not checked the history thoroughly enough to justify this notion, but I imagine if they had not *simply obeyed God*, most of these movements of the Spirit would never have come forth. (As a point of clarification - I do not believe starting over is God's ideal at all – not least on the basis of the unity we have previously discussed. If God however is seeking to move and the church leaders and structures of the day are resisting, He will initiate something new with those who are open.)

The greats of old determined: *do whatever it takes to obey God*

Jesus was a prophetic rebel

Perhaps this sounds *too strong*? Doesn't the scripture indicate "rebellion is as the sin of *witchcraft?"* (1 Sam.15:23 and *stubbornness is as idolatry* – i.e. the same as worshipping other gods.) True the Law of Moses certainly contains the strongest of punishments for the smallest *acts of rebellion* and this should prompt our humility. However, if we believe the admonition to *'not rebel'* applies to 'all rebellion' under all circumstances or as defined in the conventional fashion, it creates a significant dilemma: What of the necessity to rebel against the state when following Jesus is outlawed? How about the subversive missionaries who God aids to strengthen the underground church? (We have their stories as living testimony.) Or considering biblical history – what would have become of David who broke the law? (Mt.12:1-8) One has to wonder what Moses, Elijah, and virtually all the prophets would make of this? – *especially* since many of them suffered greatly for rebelling against man in order to obey God. We know that the kingdom is a *recipe for confrontation* with darkness! If we consider other disciples of high regard in history: what about Martin Luther and his theses? Or any of the Protestants in rebellion to the Catholic order? In fact, *we will have disqualified the majority of our reformers and revolutionaries for contradicting the official line.*

Absent clear words from God or clear moral justifications we have no basis to go against the grain. Nonetheless it seems apparent (though still surprising), that God frequently calls His people to start afresh or rebel for the sake of justice - the moral basis is commonplace, but how do we know for sure? History stands tall as our resounding witness, testifying to the common necessity. To voice new directions and ideas is hard wired into our prophetic mandate and we cannot be the voice of God without confronting the agendas of man. Prophetic messages in the Old Covenant are full of rebukes for man's rebellion against the ways of God. How often have the people had to stand as a check to misguided leadership? The paradox is therefore only resolved if we regard rebellion *against God* as the crucial issue. And so by following the Holy Spirit, we may even find ourselves in the same predicament as the first apostles:

We must obey God rather than men

Acts 5:29

I am free in every way from anyone's control

(1 Cor.9:19)

Naturally, I must add a point of clarification for the sake of those of you who do not know me so well, or have somehow missed the general sentiments of this work: I am not against organised church or peoples' commitment to it if it is fruitful and a blessing for you. Many of my friends have very positive connections with their local houses of fellowship and I am personally involved with several fellowship groups. Virtually everything God is calling us to can only be fulfilled by team and these are obvious vehicles for that. God however, *has not limited us by our church associations* – our destinies, our understanding and relationship with Him, even our ability to release the kingdom – this is the point. I believe in giving Him the full credit for working in our lives regardless of us securing some kind of 'successful' connection with 'the church,' (which can depend a great deal on others), or the supposed 'legitimacy' that this brings. So much of what God is calling us to do and be – in the workplace, preaching on the streets, family life etc. – comes from the people we are, the outflow from our relationship with Him and our initiative. Keep in mind – *no one can take from you the power of who you are*. God has invested incredible levels of authority and responsibility in the life of every believer. There is *so much* that we can do to advance the kingdom of God regardless of any official church backing. When we think upon the great potential God has laid out before us, in plain shining glory, how do we not see more fruit? *Is it time for a clean slate and some fresh breakthrough moves of the Spirit?* For sure when we see love calling, and grasp the depth of both responsibility and potential inherent in the life of all God's children, we will not be able to wait for the church to get on board before seizing the kingdom! We could even find ourselves in a place where God is so manifest among us in glory, whereby He is speaking so clearly to and through His people; that His visions are the only ones we are collectively following and the only job left for leaders, is to facilitate Him and encourage this.

Everyone is responsible before God to follow their own conscience

- Follow your conscience -

Maturity & the Discipleship of Brothers

God is able to lead His people. History is littered with the stories of saints who were personally led by God into the depths of spiritually. Their writings are a great encouragement and a treasure despite their rejection and persecution by the churches. God has repeatedly poured out His Spirit, choosing the lowly, the untrained and the uninitiated (1 Cor.1:25-31 - *so kingdom style!*) Why does He do this? It should be obvious: all things must work to the glory of God! And that no man can ever boast. Do we really think we've got it altogether and all worked out? We will always be reliant on Him. How many new moves of God are birthed in the hunger of youth? (– In that beautiful 'discovering God' phase, prior to genuine training, indoctrination or the cares of the world taking over.) Curiously, when Paul met the leaders of repute in Jerusalem, he observed *"God is not impressed with the positions men hold,"* and they *"added nothing to me"* (Gal.2:6) – God had taught Him so well, and *why not us?*

The point I am making here is not that we should not have leaders, (or that they are not a great blessing to us, or their wisdom not immensely valuable,) but that a great number of mature saints do not *need* leaders and have the capacity to be self governing, when living under the direction of the Holy Spirit accompanied with the discipleship of brothers. We should remember that leadership is established primarily because of responsibility and is needed to protect the weak, the immature and the young (even these have the Holy Spirit!) Furthermore, *nature teaches us this!* When one reaches maturity, we leave the nest thus taking on full responsibility for our lives. How many saints are waiting for their gifts and callings to be nurtured, brought forth and validated, while time flies by and God is ready to move? How many are waiting for a future time? For what or for whom? This generation lacks the number of spiritual fathers that would be needed in an ideal world to 'release' us all; God is not limited by this and the Holy Spirit has mentored a multitude, He is preparing His army!

What are we waiting for?

God is able to lead His people

The discipleship of brothers has existed as the primary means of fellowship and life for quite a number of people I know for years. Not only is it valid, it can be more effective in calling people to take responsibility for their own lives. This principle of *standing together as equals* (1 Cor.12:25, Jam.2:1 CEV) held in tandem with the principle of *open transparency*: to whosoever, *"ask me anything you like,"* provides a strong resolve to keep us on track. To adopt this principle of openness is far more humbling and vulnerable than alternatives, carrying also with it the ensuing freedom of standing in the light. Perhaps this is where public confession was intended to bring us? – Even recognising in true spiritual light the lack of truly 'private' space. So in conclusion, we are compelled at least to ask ourselves – if a council of brothers is good enough for the accountability of our leaders, surely it should be for all of us?

For those readers who continue to hold fast to a belief in the need for people to be positioned 'over' one another, consider another simple question – in what way can we intervene from 'above,' that we cannot equally intervene from standing besides? (Especially if we are working cooperatively!) The important element is having an established relationship with someone that means we both know them and are able to speak effectively into their lives. Essentially the only difference between 'above' or 'adjacent' is our perceptions about the right and authority endued on these respective positions, relating to those who have taken it upon themselves to hold us to account. What we commonly neglect to realise, is that the community has the moral right to hold any individual to account to the degree that their actions affect others. (Hence greater influence and public roles substantiate greater scrutiny.) The concept of *positional* authority does not override the intrinsic God-given *moral* authority that we all carry. (Ultimately, does not all social authority stem from this fundamental moral authority that we all carry? – this is not rhetorical, I'm asking the question...) We see clearly then, the community has much greater moral authority than we tend to believe or act upon. By rising to the call to carry the standard for righteousness and justice, having the courage to challenge each other and uphold truth and right – *we the people can raise the moral standard again in the land.*

The Holy Spirit leads us into all truth.

The churches have generally maintained for years that we are in great need of *teaching* from their leaders. What do the scriptures actually say though? And how does the church function in places of great oppression, where they are forbidden to assemble? (–like the Chinese revivals.) *We have the Word of God.* All the instruction we could ever need is written in this glorious book! And if only the saints would read the word like their lives depend on it. The great majority of messages that are preached today serve only as fresh reminders for mature believers rather than new insights; surely we should all be able to deliver these messages. What are our greatest needs? The Word, The Holy Spirit and *fellowship! The Holy Spirit leads us into all truth!* (Jn.14:26, 16:13) – do we believe this?! God Himself teaches every one of His people directly and we know His voice. I also find it curious that a great majority of messages preached would not be needed if we truly get this one principle of living in love. YES! – I absolutely believe preaching and teaching can be extremely beneficial; but our present reality is a sober one – how often would an hour of reading the Word impact us *far more* than the weak words of many of today's preachers?!

Where is the fire of God?!

The Word of God contains all the instruction we need

Spiritual Discernment & the True Believers

There is one central fear that stands against the following viewpoint from being adopted as mainstream: 'individuals following Jesus are legitimate before God (without further qualification, official associations etc.,) and we recognise them by the spirit.' (i.e. we receive them!) The fear that stands against believers implicitly trusting one another is found in the uncertainty of knowing who the true children of God are. We are unsure who to trust – who are the true believers? In our blindness we are insecure. Why do we not see the light clearly? This is an insecurity which the mature in God do not carry because we have come to trust Him to look after us, furthermore we know God is the final judge and trust Him with it. The fundamental concern is that granted too much trust or freedom, false teachers will rise up and people will be led away from Christ (or 'safety' as it is usually framed). In this context, people often reserve the right to judge one another based on their doctrine – which is a system of law not the Spirit! This law is the counterfeit to true spiritual discernment. We should all be able to discern the Spirit of God in people, and we have only sought to identify them by other means in absence of this spiritual ability. Subjecting believers to this law based *judgement* can serve to reinforce perceived boundaries and walls between the tribes and thus strikes against the unity of the Spirit. *The rejection of our brothers and sisters on these grounds must stop once for all (theology, church associations, etc.)* God has given us clear signs by which we can recognise the family: we know that we are destined to take on a striking family resemblance; not least in character, in fruit, in light and in public confession of Jesus as the Christ – it honestly isn't complicated (1 Jn.4:2). I also find it interesting to look at who Jesus trusted and to what degree – we are profoundly challenged, would we have considered these disciples 'saved' or legitimate by the usual reference frames?

Who did Jesus trust?

The desire to have structures in place as safeguards for the soul, founded in a genuine concern for the future walk of our brothers and sisters is understandable. By doing this however, we have to an extent put our faith for the protection of the soul in organisational strategies or laid the responsibility at the feet of leaders, rather than embracing the more challenging truth – *it is up to all of us to look out for each other.* More to the point – God is the ultimate protector and guardian of our souls (1 Pet.2:25, Jude 1:24). I am not writing this in opposition to safeguards, but in search for the deeper heart and sensitivity which will go even further to look out for one another. We have watched men fall, even those who had the most robust accountability strategies in place, and why? – Because people can still attempt to deceive each other and hide their sins regardless, (which is why discernment is so precious). This is true not only in spiritual circles, but these strategies have failed in a whole variety of spheres of society. The fact is, whenever a law is made and evil desire present, people attempt to find ways round it. There is no ultimate strategy which will prevent moral failures apart from the power of God – surely this is in part the message of the gospel?! So how do we respond? Do we stop trusting people? *Not at all!*

All believers should be counted worthy of our trust until such a time as they have been proven of unworthy character. The first response of our hearts to unfamiliar believers should be one of celebration and love – *we're family!* We should receive them with open arms. The greatest security we can establish against people being mislead is not institutional or law based; it is not found in making people dependent on us; but in calling *all* into maturity and discernment: freedom encourages responsibility. Every follower of Jesus must develop their own relationship with Him like a lifeline. We should only be content that they will stand through whatever comes, when we know they recognise His voice and have thoroughly absorbed His Word. Such will be evidenced by the character of Christ formed in their lives. Furthermore, *the people of God who know His Word thoroughly cannot be mislead.* The right response to this concern of God keeping His saints on track should therefore be to call the saints higher, not to seek to control them. There is no safety in the control of men.

He is the guardian of our souls.

We also observe that this fear of being mislead springs up in religious circles in response to almost every new move of the Spirit that God initiates. Again *this relates to our discernment by the Spirit;* the imperative call to us all should now be abundantly clear – we must grow our ability to discern what God is doing. When God is moving as in the glorious ways of old we cannot expect to control or oversee everything He is doing, He has not appointed us as spiritual police over His movements. Experience teaches us that not only is it beyond us, but in trying to oversee or control everything we can get in God's way! – "if it is of God, you cannot overthrow it – lest you even be found to fight against God" (Acts 5:39, or – *who was I that I could stand in God's way?* Acts.11:17). The only strategy we can embrace is to call the saints into the maturity of Christ, He is the only hope for us all.

What if a true move of God cannot be overthrown or stopped?

A People Free Under God

We have asked questions about how the relationship between saints and leaders evolves as the saints mature. How is the body of Christ to operate? The fact that God's Spirit abides in us all, and He speaks to us all and through us all, means that a significant level of cooperation will be required! What man can direct others not to pursue the call of God or ignore prophetic directives in order to serve others first? So surely one of the main purposes of our fellowship is the joining of our respective hearts, gifts and visions – for the bigger picture and to help one another, that all the things that God has laid on the hearts of His people may be expressed and pursued, and why not? Why else would He speak thus to all? Furthermore, fathers in the spirit have a particular desire for the full expression of the body of Christ to come forth – seeing that *everyone stepping into their calling* is a prerequisite to this happening (Eph.4:16, 1 Cor.12:22). We can all take great joy in serving one another's visions and seeing the fulfilment of everyone's dreams in Christ.

The mature are led by both the Spirit and love from the heart – true champions in the spirit! - Are these in need of a leader? Surely true leadership is simply to lead one another to Christ? And – *all of us are called to this!* Can we not all learn to lead (to a degree), like any skill in life? Is not the logical conclusion of effective leadership our becoming redundant since our followers have become like Christ and need us no longer? Are we free to pursue God, to conduct ourselves in love, do good deeds, and fulfil our callings without needing to consult the opinions of other men? Surely the only need the Sons of God have is for the regular fellowship of the saints? – Since they walk with God already. Will we not freely consult our brothers anyway, as those with a deep established humility know their need? In light of all this, I wonder why people are so afraid of the idea of us all being 'free under God.' Our autonomy is a God given gift. Paul even considered Himself free from every man's control, yet because of love he sought to serve everyone else and put them first! So when Jesus takes the servant heart as a foundation of maturity, is it not that He says *servants are the true leaders,* rather than *leaders happen to serve from time to time?*

We only need be sure that we have a healthy support structure around us. We are the custodians of our own lives and consciences. We have the first responsibility before God to live rightly according to that which has been entrusted to us. We alone will give full account of our lives and answer to Him for the deeds done in the body; so are we really content to look to others when the responsibility is ours? Indeed God gives men to us as gifts, great men of incredible character endued with the wisdom of years and they have our respect. Nonetheless, as we come into maturity in Christ, we will find ourselves entering *the discipleship of brothers,* and for sure it's time has come.

"And I am convinced and sure of this very thing, that He who began a good work in you will continue until the day of Jesus Christ, developing and perfecting and bringing it to full completion in you."

Phil.1:6

– Love Stories From History –

We have before us a great cloud of witnesses endued with love. In both their writings and the accounts of their lives we see such a challenge and encouragement to follow in the same way: they are examples to us. Some of the greats who have gone before us have been literally compared to Jesus by people who knew them: people who met them saw so much of God in them, so much beautiful character and such a full heart of love that they were considered to be true *Christians*.

Occasionally we are graced with meeting one of the Lord's love champions here on earth – those so in love with Him, overflowing in spirit, gentle, gracious, attentive, loving, patient – we have seen the real substance of *someone who looks and walks like Jesus* here now.

Paul: The Servant of All

Paul is clearly one of the best examples we have of love, as communicated through his writings. What follows is a brief study on his heart revealed and expressed. People are generally more struck by Paul's revelations and theology than his love, true he talks more of theology than love, but His love is so strongly communicated in his letters it is profoundly striking. The characteristics of someone both in love with God and His family are clearly displayed:

A burning desire for all to come to their fullest potential in God

"Him we preach and proclaim, warning and admonishing everyone and instructing everyone in all wisdom, that we may present every person mature in Christ. For this I labour [unto weariness], striving with all the superhuman energy which He so mightily enkindles and works within me."

Col.1:28-29

He also considered that his calling was to *'enlighten all men'* (Eph.3:9), without distinction.

Wishing to suffer in the place of others

"I am speaking the truth in Christ, I am not lying; my conscience [enlightened and prompted] by the Holy Spirit bearing witness with me that I have bitter grief and incessant anguish in my heart. For I could wish that I myself were accursed and cut off and banished from Christ for the sake of my brethren and instead of them, my natural kinsmen and my fellow countrymen."

Rom.9:1-3

Praying with his whole heart

"Brethren with all my heart's desire and goodwill for [Israel], I long and pray to God that they may be saved."

Rom.10:1

Yearning

"I keep pleading that somehow by God's will I may now at last prosper and come to you. For I am yearning to see you, that I may impart and share with you some spiritual gift to strengthen and establish you; that is, that we may be mutually strengthened and encouraged and comforted by each other's faith, both yours and mine."

Rom.1:10-12

"...My brethren whom I love and yearn to see, my delight and crown... my beloved."

Phil.4:1

And yet, when yearning to be with Christ, his love for the Philippians caused him to choose to stay on earth:

"My yearning desire is to depart and be with Christ, but to remain in my body is more needful and essential for your sake."

Phil.1:23-25

"And they yearn for you while they pray for you, because of the surpassing measure of God's grace in you."

2 Cor.9:14

"That is the reason that, when I could bear [the suspense no longer], I sent that I might learn [how you were standing the strain], and the endurance of your faith, [for I was fearful] lest somehow the tempter had tempted you...

Timothy has just come back to us from [his visit to] you and has brought us the good news of [the steadfastness of] your faith and [the warmth of your] love, and [reported] how kindly you cherish a constant and affectionate remembrance of us [and that you are] longing to see us as we [are to see] you."

1 Thes.3:5, 6

Teaching them everything that would benefit them, holding nothing back

"How I did not shrink from telling you anything that was for your benefit..."

Acts 20:20

"For I never shrank or kept back or fell short from declaring to you the whole purpose and plan and counsel of God."

Acts 20:27

His work was tireless and unceasing; he took the time to counsel the people one on one

"Therefore be always alert and on your guard, being mindful that for three years I never stopped night or day seriously to admonish and advise and exhort you one by one with tears!"

Acts 20:31

He literally experienced *love* as the most empowering and moving force in his life

"For the love of Christ controls and urges and impels us"

2 Cor.5:14

He wrote to the Corinthians to show them he loved them, and this love was growing!

"For I wrote you out of great sorrow and deep distress of heart, with many tears, not to cause you pain but in order to make you realize the overflowing love that I continue increasingly to have for you."

2 Cor.2:4*

The extreme love of a radical heart

"Yes, furthermore, I count everything as loss compared to the possession of the priceless privilege of knowing Christ Jesus my Lord and of progressively becoming more deeply and intimately acquainted with Him. For His sake I have lost everything and consider it all to be mere rubbish (refuse, dregs), in order that I may win Christ.

[For my determined purpose is] that I may know Him, and that I may in that same way come to know the power outflowing from His resurrection, and that I may so share His sufferings as to be continually transformed to His death. That if possible I may attain to the resurrection out from among the dead."

Phil.3:8, 10-11*

A love that counts all things loss for the sake of knowing a loved one more; a love that craves deeper fellowship even through the greatest suffering; such is a love unmatched.

Continually thanking God for them, in every memory of them

He talks of these followers of Jesus who have a love for all the saints and how proud he is of them and grateful he is to God in light of this love and faith.

"We ought and indeed are obligated to give thanks always to God for you, brethren, as is fitting, because your faith is growing exceedingly and the love of every one of you each toward the others is increasing and abounds."

2 Thes.1:3*

A community of people all growing in love without exception?!

WOW. I cannot find the words!

"I thank God in all my remembrance of you."

Phil.1:3-4, Col.1:3-4, Eph.1:15-16

"And besides these things that are without, there is the daily [inescapable pressure] of my care and anxiety for all the churches!"

2 Cor.11:28

Who stumbles and I am not on fire?!

2 Cor.11:29

Paul feels the empathy of them all, the weight of care for all the churches, and not a day went by when he didn't feel it – having personally glimpsed this and felt the Lord's heart for all His people – words cannot describe the depth of it, like seeing His majesty, it leaves us undone.

Paul prays for the Philippians

"It is right and appropriate for me to have this confidence and feel this way about you all, because you have me in your heart and I hold you in my heart as partakers and sharers, one and all with me... for God is my witness how I long for and pursue you all with love, in the tender mercy of Christ Jesus [Himself]! And this I pray: that your love may abound yet more and more and extend to the fullest development in knowledge and all keen insight [that your love may display itself in greater depth of acquaintance and more comprehensive discernment], so that you may surely learn to sense what is vital, and approve and prize what is excellent and of real value [recognizing the highest and the best, and distinguishing the moral differences], and that you may be untainted and pure and unerring and blameless [so that with hearts sincere and certain and unsullied, you may approach the day of Christ not stumbling or causing others to stumble]. May you abound in and be filled with the fruits of righteousness..."

Phil.1:7-11

Such a clear full hearted message of care to the Thessalonians: The first letter.

*"Being affectionately desirous of you, we continued to share with you not only God's good news but **also our own lives as well** for you had become so very dear to us (2:8)." We behaved gently when we were among you, like a devoted mother nursing and cherishing her own children" (2:7). Worked night and day in order to never become a burden (9). As a father dealing with his own children we used to exhort each of you personally" (11).*

1 Thes.2:7-11, emphasis added

"For what thanksgiving can we render to God for you for all the gladness and delight which we enjoy for your sakes before our God? [And we] continue to pray especially and with most intense earnestness night and day that we may see you face to face and mend and make good whatever may be imperfect and lacking in your faith."

I Thes.3:9-10*

"And may the Lord make you to increase and excel and overflow in love for one another and for all people, just as we also do for you. So that He may strengthen and confirm and establish your hearts faultlessly pure and unblamable in holiness in the sight of our God and Father, at the coming of our Lord Jesus Christ with all his saints Amen!"

1 Thes.3:12-13*

"Because now we [really] live, if you stand [firm] in the Lord"

I Thes.3:8

And lastly of Timothy, he was exemplary because he truly carried the Spirit of Christ

"For I have no one like him [no one of so kindred a spirit] who will be so genuinely interested in your welfare and devoted to your interests. For the others all seek [to advance] their own interests, not those of Jesus Christ."

Phil.2:20-21*

– Meditations –

To paint fresh pictures –

in visions of spiritual love that inspire the heart to life:

here is our [creative] mission.

Our entire mandate –

to manifest the fathers love in all creation

A vision for the oneness of God manifest in
humanity

We are a people destined to become love.

Get ready to become the biggest hearted
people on earth

A lot more love would make a massive difference to EVERYTHING

The harmony God seeks to establish is by no means monochrome, we are made to be an eclectic mish mash of beautiful lovers intertwined on this spiritual journey and as our paths cross we hold hands and dive further in.

The genius of a holiness movement set on love:
All we have to find is this one thing-
How we keep love alive, active and growing...

Stronger together: the power of union

"If possible...

...live at peace with everyone"
Rom.12:18

Love is the greatest testimony
Love is the greatest victory

If we spend a life learning love

we will not be disappointed

If we do this, how can we fail?

AND: how can we fail to see *all* the glories of God?

...The coming of His very kingdom

"For whatever a man sows that and that only is what he will reap."

Gal.6:7

Only faith working through love counts for anything

~ Gal.5:6

God has given us a fearless Spirit

God has given us a Spirit of love: full of power

2 Tim.1:7

Few have mastered love

What if a generation does?

In times gone by, the moves of God were marked by particular revelations, repentance, miracles or the presence of God...

...Is it not time for the move of God that is marked by love?!

When love rains down: do we drink it all up and share it around?

What if we loved people so much that they genuinely believed that we would love them whatever happened?

Teach the world to love

this is our calling.

Beloved, if God loved us so [very much],

we also ought to love one another.

1 Jn.4:11

Loving people is the adventure of Christ

What if we were so frequently moved by compassion,

it possessed us?

I have loved you with an everlasting love

A friend loves at all times.

God, may we become your best friends.

There is one who will never betray you.

I HAVE CHOSEN YOU

Eph.1:4, John.15:16

Love champions

God was supremely wise
- choosing love as His primary tactic
this is no weak strategy.

Wherever my presence is, there you should be

Love is to be the hallmark of the followers of Jesus

"Let everything you do be done in love."

1 Cor.16:14

Love does no wrong to one's neighbour - It never hurts anybody

Rom.13:10

Let our lives lovingly express truth in all things

Enfolded in love, let us grow up in every way
and in all things unto Him who is the head
Eph.4:15

Before us are limitless skies

1 Jn.3:1 SEE what an incredible quality of love the Father has given us – see it!

SEE IT!

"There is no fear in love"
1 John 4:18

The Spirit loves freely

– Closing Thoughts –

God is on the move! Glory!

My sincere hope is that the power and potential of His love has gripped your heart as you've been reading this book. I pray that He will open the depths of the experiences we have explored and make the deepest truths real to your heart. In examining the dynamics of what love truly is, from the individual to the community, I have tried to cover anything that could be helpful and relevant to us walking out this journey. By looking at the Word of God in great detail, we have an indisputable case for this notion that our lives are truly all about love and knowing God.

I put it to you also, that now being aware of God's heart and intentions we also have no reason to divide any longer. Perhaps in this little glimpse we have started to comprehend the dynamic power of tribes standing together. As beautiful as well formed communities are, they will rarely win a war alone: especially in a battle in which one of our most powerful weapons is *our standing together*. Satan knows that if we are divided and fighting one another, we are distracted from our purpose and by it we inhibit the power of God. The moment we stand together and walk forward, the battle is over.

We are simply free to love, evermore.

And so our final prayer:

"May the Lord direct your hearts into the love of God."

2 Thes.3:5

– Credits & Thanks –

I cannot express my gratitude enough: To my parents, Steve & Tricia: for being such loving characters, for keeping to your convictions and high standards, for teaching me in the ways of God, for supporting me through difficult circumstances, for your efforts in helping me produce this work. To my closest friends: for sticking by me while for years I strayed, for loving me through all my quirks, for encouraging me to do this and for really believing in me – Scot, Mark & Mark, Simon, Jon, Mikko. To the fathers who have inspired me along the way: Geoff, Rod and Rick. To all my proof readers – for their patience, diligence and their invaluable input. To Mark & Dan for giving me the final nudge that I needed – to do what I had been avoiding for a long time... To Heidi & Roland for daring to live the message and holding to it whatever happens. Thank you all so much, you made this happen. Let's hope it was worth it!

– Appendices –

Appendix 1: Personal Review

People have adopted all kinds of lists - 'righteousness checkups', accountability cards, tackling the various issues of life. Regardless of what one thinks about the merits or otherwise of doing this, I am yet to hear of any groups of people engaged in 'accountability questions' that ask each other how well are we 'walking in love?' perhaps surprising considering how clear and strong Jesus is on this.

Do people feel loved by me?

How can I show them more love?

How can I seize more opportunities for love?

Am I acting in love towards those outside my usual circles?

Am I loving God?

Is He my first love?

Appendices

Appendix 2: Practical Essentials

Whilst my intention was never to make this a manual per se, or delve too much into practical wisdom, there are a small number of simple principles which help to establish healthy and respectful relationships: to treat people honourably and properly. It seemed appropriate to include this brief summary of practical guidelines for community living. I am still regularly astounded by the behaviour of many believers, who *act so often without thinking* of others; yet with their mouths utter such empty words of respect. Often it is simply insensitivity and a lack of *learning to think of others* in all of our actions, yet there is no excuse (we give grace nonetheless). People may have made a mental agreement with the basic principles outlined below; but being consistent, fully thinking through and working through these principles, and what they look like practically – this a wholly different ball game. Some believers have brought the Lord's name into such disrepute and so dishonoured their fellow brethren that people even refuse to trade with Christians any more – or others have become so offended and hurt through the actions of Christians and Churches – often leaders, that they wish to find no association with us any more – this is such a lamentable state! It is even a well known precept in working spheres that Christians can be the worst to work for: not paying their bills on time, always haggling for cheap prices and expecting everything for free. It may be the gospel to the poor and we may not have much; but God forbid we try to rip everyone else off and so discredit everything we say we believe.

Ground Rules

(The bare minimum)

1. *To treat others as we wish to be treated* – and of course, consider other peoples' value systems, if their standards are higher, we may need to go the extra mile beyond what we believe is sufficient or appropriate. Not only – *how would our actions make us feel if we were in their position*? but, if we were actually the other person, and wired the way that they are – *how would they feel*? It can make so much difference when we learn to empathise and fully understand the perspectives of others and the reasons for them. Recognising the validity of alternative views is an essential part of respect. **Thinking things through is an essential element to practical love**: we become more sensitive and therefore more observant to the needs and desires of others; we consider well the impacts of all our actions.

2. *To always pay our way* – this includes not expecting things for free, not taking gifts for granted, clearing our debts as soon as possible and not creating liabilities for other people. We have had many guests at our home in recent years, and we have wanted to offer our support during their stay with us and give it for free; but we have changed our community approach in order to set the right precedent: so that people are never presumptuous and to always attempt to cover our costs, that our culture will be to never become a burden on others. Some people will willingly suffer for others, and cover costs they cannot truly afford; we should not allow them to do this. Essentially, we should assume to pay a fair rate, unless some other arrangement is made. Everyone should contribute in some way, *if we do not work, should we eat? Should we take bread for nothing? Ok so you've bought your own food, but what about the gas bill for that shower you took earlier?* Furthermore, in regard to loaning, borrowing, sharing – people often create liabilities and small debts, in the promise of repayment later. We have had to acknowledge that people aren't always the best at managing their affairs honourably. We should seek to clear any debts we create *as soon as possible* – no one should have to chase their debts, it is the responsibility of the borrowers to settle their accounts! Not only this, we should be careful not to create liabilities for other people by being thoughtless or careless – find out the full cost of things, life can have many hidden costs! Drivers particularly will be able to identify with these experiences – the amount that they give in *free fuel (and what of their time?);* but even when fuel is paid, is anyone thinking about a little extra for maintenance and insurance? We really should make sure we go beyond the minimum in this and expect nothing for free! It always costs someone.

3. *To always clear up and clean up after ourselves – leaving places as we would wish to find them.* Just to be clear – leaving them clean, tidy and presentable. One of the biggest causes of tension in a household is the sense of people not pulling their weight. There are disagreements about standards and what is appropriate. In our experience, the highest standard should be adopted and maintained; else it always falls to the lowest common denominator – the lowest standard of what someone else is prepared to put up with, until they get desperate! For me, one thing that profoundly changed my approach was a desire to be

hospitable and welcoming – *we always want to do the best for our guests*, and *we want our guests to be able to turn up any time.* There is no longer therefore a discussion about who's standard is sufficient as if we are tidying for ourselves, we are doing it for others – this can be a game changer!

4. *Keep our word* – if we pledge to do anything, we must stick to it – or ask to be let out of the agreement (Mt.5:33-37). Sticking to what we have promised is a basic way of building trust, without which it is near impossible to work with people.

5. *Be on time* – this one is probably the biggest personal challenge, especially as a bit of John 3:8 – working with the spontaneous ebs and flows of life can make it tough! (To say the least.) Nonetheless *being on time* is for some folks an absolute standard of honour – a lot of people won't understand or accept any number of reasons or excuses (are we making dishonest excuses or shifting blame?); blaming the Lord for making you late is rarely helpful! I understand there are times when being late can be legitimate, but if in any doubt; it is best that we communicate to determine the etiquette and expectations in any given scenario. Honour all men!

6. *Take responsibility* – for communal things, if in doubt or the situation is unclear we should take responsibility. One of the biggest failings of social experiments and socialism in general, is the lack of participation and responsibility taken by people in regard to the collectively owned. Unfortunately those who advocate private ownership on the grounds of *'it will be better looked after and utilised,'* can often make a strong case. *The property of everyone is the property of no one...* perhaps. This state of affairs does not have to exist. The default assumption that people often make is that everything is *someone else's job* or responsibility – and so leave things alone. Situations can arise where everyone claims *no responsibility* – and perhaps it always gets left to a certain person to pick up the pieces. We later discover a guest accidentally made an error – for which we should all have grace! How about the opposite situation? – *where any discrepancy is dealt with quickly and responsibly by any and all* – this will help maintain a good, clean environment and prevent many a disagreement. The habit of human nature may cause us to

overestimate our contribution, underestimate our responsibilities and leave jobs for others. This is not the way of Christ!

7. *Sort relational issues out as soon as possible* – so we've been trying to follow the above, but somehow we've still had an argument, fallen out, let people down etc. Jesus was abundantly clear that we should sort out any issues as soon as possible, that we should make the effort to go first to our brother or sister, even if the error was clearly theirs (Mt.5:23-24, Eph.4:26).

8. *Maybe we should seek first the kingdom as well?!*

Appendix 3: Cooperative Leadership

Why are participation and a shared sense of ownership key to effective leading?

Cooperation is preferable where possible, but why?

(there are also exceptions to this principle due to practical circumstances)

When we extend responsibility to others there is a much greater chance of them valuing and owning something – we invite them to participate and by this we are demonstrating we value them. We recognise that people feel a true sense of ownership over things that they have influence over and that this enables us to fully throw our hearts in. Developing a collective sense of ownership is about hearts coming together, the community becoming the most vibrant it can be. This is why a cooperative model is preferable and can be both more effective and more loving. The gifts of the multitude should be utilised for the good of the many. Dreaming as a community can create the kind of social cohesion needed to shift the social breakdown and separation caused by the individualism of recent decades. True, everyone should be encouraged to pursue the visions that God places on their heart as and when they are able to. But how many of our dreams are for the communities we are here to serve and sent to help? Are we in and among them? Do we know their heart beats and their needs? Surely a pragmatic solidarity grounds our dreams in real people and real issues? If I have your back and you have mine, and I dream for you and you dream for me; we can all be selfless while pursuing the dreams of God's heart.

As to the outworking of our collective dreaming and responsibility: there are works of the kingdom that will require a great company of people mobilised to accomplish, we need to identify the times when we need to prioritise coming together for the greater good. From a pragmatic perspective, we will not be able to do everything, but the Holy Spirit is here to assist us in finding our way forward!

The practical benefits of cooperative arrangements are many. Not least the reduction of responsibility resting on those who are facilitating or overseeing. Those who lead projects often battle an overly strong sense of ownership and responsibility, whilst sometimes frustrated that others neglect to see themselves as stakeholders, consequently not becoming involved. We will therefore do well to encourage a strong team ethic, invite contributions and ideas, and empower people to lead themselves (and each other) rather than be dependent on leaders 'above' them. We have found that followers of Jesus rarely take a strong personal sense of ownership over anything God is doing, absent Him revealing His heart for it to them; we need clear vision to be able to embrace it (Pr.29:18). Our job as visionaries is to clearly expound both the visions and heart of God in all the fire and passion He speaks them to us; to see the visions released in an atmosphere of the anointing, and to create a space for Him to speak to us, so that the people hear *His heart* and *His voice*. Our hearts are moved by His voice; He has designed us to operate from our hearts. We also know that God is most glorified in each individual when they are expressing Christ as fully as they are able, in the specific ways they have been created to - this looks different for all of us. The visions of God released through a diverse group will *always* be expressed differently. *God is NOT making clones of us!*

Appendix 4: Keeping an Open Heart

We have considered the dynamic of an open heart and how this can be rooted in love. When contemplating how to keep our hearts in this place of freedom, it is beneficial to understand the nature of the heart, mind and soul of man: How are we wired? What events in life affect us? How do we process and understand what we see and hear? How can we best steward our hearts and minds? And more specifically, what it is that causes our hearts to close down or become hard?

We have already established in earlier chapters how much affect the Spirit and love of God have on our hearts; my intention is therefore not to cover this again. There are however, a number of different ways people process what is going on their hearts, it may help therefore to briefly cover this in more detail.

For starters, a free heart does not hold on to anything, and does not carry baggage. In order to come to this place, we must first commit everything to the lord, in true surrender: trust Him with our hopes and dreams (look to Him in all things), let go of our disappointments (and our pessimism – if relevant); keep short accounts (confess our sins) and continually walk in forgiveness. Trusting Him with our lives is the foundation of peace in this respect. Our minds must be renewed by the truth, thus producing the consequential change in our expectations with lasting resolve. We need to know He is trustworthy and has good plans in order to truly release our lives to Him and dispel any fears.

The degree of freedom that we find may depend on our expectations for life. If we have come to Jesus, but our worldview has not been conformed to the kingdom, our hopes may not be fulfilled; they may even become a source of conflict between us and His plans for us. In simple terms, complete surrender leading to trust is the basis of a free heart before God: this is part of the foundation of *faith toward God* (Heb.6:1).

We begin by being real – honesty, is a pre-requisite to our finding wholeness. Just as with any relationship communication is paramount, and the Lord loves honesty. Whenever we struggle to let go, we can ask Him for help, for revelation, for reassurance. The first place of trust we come to is our decision to engage in dialogue with Him over the state of our hearts, often He does the rest. We need to continually commit ourselves to God, because every day we face new opportunities, decisions and challenges – daily choices and daily battles! If this were not so, we could make a one-off commitment and be done with it. This is also the basis for our continual confession of sins – even on the most basic level, *this is right relationship:* we sort things out when things come between us.

As regards the various approaches for *guarding the heart, the wellspring of life* (Pr.4:23), we know that feeding our hearts and minds the truth of God's Word is essential. Dealing with issues as soon as possible – *when they spring up*, is the most effective way of preventing impact or lasting damage on our hearts (– *nip it in the bud.*) Keeping short accounts with God is therefore an obvious strategy: whether it be a personal daily discipline, part of a weekly gathering, or when taking regular communion. Regular times of deep fellowship in the presence of the Lord have been for me a greater key to walking in freedom than any regime one adopts to keep oneself in check; His presence transforms us and where the Spirit of the Lord is there is freedom! (2 Cor.3:17). Grace abounds in His presence. As we become more like Him: in patience, in grace: we become difficult to offend – it is harder for the things of life to impact us in a negative fashion and there is far less for us to deal with or to resolve.

In more recent times, folks have been engaging in frequent *'sozo'* sessions (as pioneered by Bethel Church in the U.S.): to create a space for God to deal with anything that has come between us and Him. These sessions are set up in such a way as to be led by the Holy Spirit (via prophetic insights from the team). Often the specific focus falls on dealing with unhealed wounds, errant belief systems (conscious or otherwise), and the release of fresh words of hope and promise. Why is this effective, and is it really necessary? Due to our nature – how we are wired, we do not always realise how situations have affected us until we bring them before the Lord. Determination of *how we are to hold our hearts before Him* is informed by us truly knowing ourselves and being aware of what affects us. We have a relatively strong basis (from understanding the nature of the heart,) for engaging in some kind of *regular open time* with God – for Him to highlight anything we may need to deal with. Considering how integral regular physical disciplines are to life, is it any surprise spiritual disciplines can be powerful for all? Of course there is nothing to prevent us having these conversations with God at any time in our own way; in fact, adopting the stance – *I want nothing between You and me Lord, let's deal with anything and everything as soon as possible* – is probably best (- seriously, there is nothing to be afraid of and no reason not to deal with issues as soon as possible, people are sometimes reluctant, but it is largely without foundation. God deals with things and we find ourselves often surprised how gentle He is and how easy it can be to let go).

So why doesn't He do it all instantly, or why retain our need to process? Apparently His wisdom saw fit to do it this way. We are people made in His image, in His form! We were made for a journey of discovery (Pr.25:2?) God seems to have created life as *a journey of the heart*, a dialogue centred on developing relationships. We find life in discovering and *knowing Him* more. Our choices and challenges are important, and He is interested in our story. We also place much greater value on that which truly costs us. Perhaps this is why He is revealing Himself *to us* and *in us 'in part,'* (little by little,) and we see more of His glory as the Great Day approaches. Becoming ever more transformed into the likeness of His nature. The most beautiful of days is coming ever so soon, in which we – *His family – will finally be completely transformed into His likeness in the twinkle of an eye...*

I can't wait!